TURQUOISE CAPRIS AND PEACH DAIQUIRIS

A Little Lexicon of Words Derived From Places

Steven Gilbar

INTRODUCTION

This discursive little volume corrals words that are derived from the proper names of places. They are, that is, toponyms, defined in the *American Heritage Dictionary* as "any name derived from a place or region." They range from the obvious, such as *china* and *hamburger*, to the obscure, such as *hafnium* and *rockaway*. Not every such word has been included here— the names of cheeses and wines alone could fill a volume.*

Purposely excluded are names from literature and the Bible, as they are gathered in an earlier book of mine, *Catch-22; or Babbit*: A Lilliputian Lexicon of Literary Eponyms. What is presented are familiar words that, often surprisingly, have a topographic origin, such as *copper* and *denim*, and words that are not exactly common, but have interesting place name etymologies, such as *jodhpurs* and *solecism*. The selection process may seem capricious—it is; not trying to be comprehensive, I have been able to pick words that I found interesting. I have tried to limit entries to single words rather than compound words such as *Belgian endive* or *Venetian*

---

* With a few exceptions I have not included any culinary words. They can be found in my *Chicken a la King and the Buffalo Wing:* Food Names and the People and Places that Inspired Them.

blinds; however, I have reserved the right to use some that I thought you might like.

The words are arranged alphabetically and are made up of definition, etymology, and an example of usage. As this is not a serious academic work, many of the examples of use are limericks and other doggerel of my own devising, for which I take full responsibility.

I do not profess to be a professor or a professional etymologist; rather, I am, like you, one who loves the English language and has been rambling through it for many years, serendipitously discovering along the way curious word origins. I also am interested in geography, so that when language and place intersect, such as with toponyms, I experience a frisson of pleasure. How else explain my satisfaction in discovering that the *daiquiri* is named after a beach in Cuba or that *magenta* is named for a famous battle site in Italy. It is my hope that in delving in this collection you will experience a similar delight.

A

ABYSSINIAN

The Abyssinian, one of the oldest cat breeds, does not take its name because it originated in Abyssinia (present-day Ethiopia), but because the first of its kind exhibited in England in the 1820s was supposedly imported from there. Its actual provenance is unknown. A gladiolus, the **Abyssinian Sword Lily,** and the **Abyssinian Primrose** are also from Ethiopia, as is the **Abyssinian Roller**, a bird, and the misleadingly-named **Abyssinian Banana** (it does not produce an edible fruit).

> An Abyssinian cat called Riba, a name
> Penny had derived from some mystic
> experiment, stared with greenish yellow
> eyes from a tree branch, crouched as if
> to pounce on anyone walking in the
> path below.
> Patricia Highsmith, *Mermaids
> On the Golf Course* (1985)

ACADEMY

It is derived from *Akademia*, the place where Plato taught in ancient Athens. It was not a building, but a grove-filled public park in one of the city's toniest suburbs. "Academe" is what academicians call the place where they work when they are feeling grand. "Academic," in the sense of "not leading to a decision," did not come into use until the nineteenth century.

> Since she couldn't be an academic, she'd
> decided to continue working on the academic
> novel she'd begun in Bloomington, and to
> that end had been compiling descriptions of
> English Department Types.
> Haven Kimmel, *The Solace of
> Leaving Early* (2002)

ADIRONDACK CHAIR

A man named Thomas Lee invented the famous outdoor chair in 1903 at his summer home in Westport, New York, on the edge of Lake Champlain, by the Adirondack Mountains. He showed it to a local carpenter who, without Lee's knowledge, secured a patent on it, calling it a "Westport chair." Over time it became better known as the "Adirondack chair."

> She came back with a glass of wine and
> sat beside him in the other green Adirondack
> chair. They rarely sat in these chairs, which
> held their places on the lawn through
> summer and winter, patient as old souls.
> Christopher Tilghman, *Roads
> Of the Heart* (2004)

AFGHAN

The names of the shawl, the carpet, and the hound all stem from their place of origin--Afghanistan.

> "A white guy's got about as much chance of
> getting in and out of that place undetected and
> alive as an elephant's got knitting an afghan."
> Bill Kelly & Dolph Le Moult,
> *Dream Street* (1989)

AFRICAN VIOLET

The popular houseplant—officially *Saintpaulia ionantha*--is not a violet at all. The genus name is a shortened version of its discoverer, Baron Walter Von Saint Paul-Illaire—who brought the seeds back to Europe from the mountains of East Africa in 1892—while the species name is Greek and means having flowers like violets. Hence the popular name: African violet.

> In a north window African violets thrive and
> bring us their brilliant tints. Did you ever
> look at an African violet flower closely? The
> rich velvety blue is a magnificent tone, and
> the bloom itself a work of art and well worth
> studying with a magnifying glass.
> Jean Hersey, *The Shape of a Year*
> (1967)

AFRO

The name for the full "halo" hairstyle comes from Afro—the combining form of "African." It is often shortened to "fro" or called a "natural. In the 1960s it expanded to become a general adjective for black styles of clothing, music, and the like.

> The "afro" in the late 1960s became almost
> synonymous with the Civil Rights movement.
> The style was worn s a mark of defiance against
> inappropriate white beauty myths, signifying a
> rejection of the embedded beliefs that Afro hair
> was something to be intrinsically ashamed of.
> Michael Wintle, *Image and Identity*
> (2006)

AGARIC

The mushroom, with its gills and umbrella-like cap, is of the genus *Agricus*, meaning "from Agara," an area of Eastern Europe once known as Samartia, part of the Scythian empire.

Fly agaric (*amanita muscaria*), a red and white spotted toadstool, is associated with fairies that are often depicted sitting on one.

> The fly agaric is very beautiful, it grows
> in plantations in autumn, and looks like
> a round crimson satin cushion stuck with
> white-headed pins. They delight in damp,
> and what we should call unwholesomeness.
> Charlotte Mary Yonge, *The Herb
> of the Field* (1887)

AGATE

A common variety of chalcedony quartz used often in jewelry, it comes from the Achates River in Sicily, known today as the Dirillo. Along its upper course Greeks and, later, Romans, found it and exported it throughout the Mediterranean region. "Agate" is the English translation of the Greek *Achates*.

> Is it, then, evening
> So soon? I see, the night-dews,
> Cluster'd in thick beads, dim
> The agate brooch-stones
> On thy white shoulder;
> From "The Strayed Reveler"
> (1849) by Matthew Arnold

AIREDALE

The Airedale, the largest of all terrier breeds, originated in the Valley of Aire in the County of York, England.

> When my Airedale died I crawled
> into the dark
> doghouse and lay down as the ghost
> of him ran through me. . . .
> From "Zephyr" by Timothy
> Muskat (1996)

AKITA

This breed is thought to have developed in Akita Prefecture, located in the north of Honshu Island, facing the Sea of Japan.

> In the 1930s, the great Helen Keller—blind and deaf since infancy but nevertheless amazingly accomplished—was given an Akita by the Emperor of Japan. She was the first American to acquire this stunning breed, the hometown dog of Japan.
> Callie Smith Grant, *The Dog Next Door* (2011)

ALEPPO PINE

This evergreen is found in the Mediterranean area, including Aleppo, Syria, where it was first described. Curiously, there the most dominant pine is the **Brutian pine**—referring to "Bruttium," the ancient name for the Italian region of Calabria. The Aleppo is the most commonly planted tree in Israel where it is called **Jerusalem pine**.

> Spétse works like smelling salts; it's a corpse reviver, a spiritually renewing slap on the bottom. And every year, as the hydrofoil from Athens approaches the island and that first whiff of Aleppo pines comes blasting across the sea, some deep part of me starts to stretch and yawn and shake itself awake, happy to find itself back home.
> Isabella Tree, "Spétses" (2001)

ALLEMANDE

A dance generally offered as a standard portion in a musical suite, as it is one of the most popular dances of the Baroque genre. Its origin can be traced down to the Renaissance period in the sixteenth century when *allemande* was the French word for "German." **Allemande left** is a square dance movement where two facing dancers take left hands or forearms, turn halfway around to the left, let go, and step forward.

> Around 1620, the four-part suite,
> consisting of the allemande, courante,
> sarabande, and gigue, replaced the
> two-part suite. . . . . The allemande,
> a couple dance performed at court,
> began in Germany.
> > Gayle Kassing, *History of
> > Dance* (2007)

ALPINE

Of or relating to high mountains. Used in mountaineering and skiing; for example, "alpine skiing" refers to competitive downhill or slalom events. In biology it refers to species living or growing on mountains above the timberline. The word is derived from "the Alps," the great European mountain range.

> In the tearooms and afternoon dance-bars
> in the little groups that huddled round the
> English notice-board at the end of the day's
> skiing, his prowess as an alpinist was
> deferentially admired.
> > John Le Carré, *The Naïve and
> > Sentimental Lover* (19710

ALSATIAN

The Alsatian—what the British call the German Shepherd (*Deutscher Schaferhund*)—did not originate in Alsace. It seems that right after the First World War, a few of the dogs were taken to England and renamed "Alsatian Shepherds" because of the prevailing anti-German sentiments. It was not until 1977 that the British Kennel Club authorized the breed to be known once more as the German Shepherd.

> There are no Dragons in the parish of St.
> George. Just the Alsatian dogs . . . that the
> rich people keep. Dogs that can tear your
> guts out, and your heart out, if they catch
> you on the wrong side of the road.
> Austin Clarke, *The Polished
> Hoe* (2004)

AMERICANO

In Europe, an espresso with hot water came to be called an "Americano" or "Caffe Americano," probably because of the American preference for weak brews. Some believe that it came from American soldiers in occupied Italy during World War II who would ask for their coffees to be watered down to more closely resemble what they considered real coffee

> Bond ordered an Americano and examined
> the sprinkling of overdressed customers,
> mostly from Paris he guessed, who sat
> talking with focus and vivacity. . . .
> Ian Fleming, *Casino Royale* (1953)

AMONTILLADO

The name of the pale dry sherry indicates its place of origin, meaning in Spanish "made in Montilla," Spain.

> He asked for a glass of Amontillado,
> but then, in the presence of this dry,
> pale wine, the gentle lenitives, the
> soothing stories of the English author
> vanished and in their place appeared
> the harsh revulsives, the painful skin
> irritants of Edgar Allan Poe; the
> chilling nightmare of the cask of
> Amontillado . . .

J, K. Huysmans, *Against Nature* (1884)

ANGLO

In the United States, the non-technical term "Anglo" has come to mean a non-Hispanic white person. Unfortunately, many who fit that category find "Anglo" offensive, especially those whose ancestry is not English, as the term--short for "Anglo-American"—means literally an American whose forbears came from England and is derived from "Anglia," the name given to the English by the Romans.

> Vera was no longer a Saldivia but a Vidal,
> and with that misleading last name she
> could fool anyone into thinking she was
> some middle-aged Anglo woman who had
> a taste for shopping on Fifth Avenue
>   Ernesto Quinonez, *Bodega
>   Dreams* (2000)

ANGORA

Angora wool or fiber refers to the downy coat produced by the Angora rabbit. While their names are similar, Angora fiber is distinct from that which comes from the Angora goat. The rabbits are believed to have originated in Turkey, along with the Angora cat and goat. "Angora" was the name of the city of Ankara and the surrounding province in Turkey prior to 1930.

> There was a lady from Turkey
> Whose bunny was quite quirky.
> The angora rabbit
> Had the bad habit
> Of drinking the woman's best
>   whiskey.

14

ANGOSTURA

Both the bitters—the single most widely distributed bar item in the world—and the aromatic bark of certain South American trees take their name from the Orinoco river town of Angostura in Venezuela—changed to "Ciudad Bolivar" in the 1840s.

> As for Angostura bitters, I have memories of my dad's bar where that curious little paper-wrapped bottle was tipped carefully over a sugar cube, which was crushed meticulously with a mulling stick to make what I'm certain was a perfect old-fashioned. My childhood fascination ended with the aroma of the bitters, which was strangely akin to mincemeat. The tiniest drop on the tongue explained its name.
>
> Barbara Witt, *The Weekend Chef* (2003)

ANTIMACASSAR

A small crocheted cloth, a doily, used on the back of sofas and chairs to protect against Macassar oil, once a popular hair pomade in Victorian England. Macassar (or "Makassar") is a port city on the island of Sulawesi in Indonesia, where the ingredients of the oil are reputed to have been manufactured.

> He deposited himself in a rocking chair draped with a starched antimacassar which scraped unpleasantly against the pink fold of skin above his collar
>
> Edith Wharton, *The House of Mirth* (1905)

APPALOOSA

The horse with the spotted coat is the result of breeding by the Nez Percé Indians of the Pacific Northwest. Its name comes from the Palouse River, which runs through the region.

> Oh what a beautiful sight to behold,
> To watch the graceful horse's running
> unfold,
> Such joy is bliss beyond what can ever
> be told,
> When an appaloosa would not be sold.
> From "Appaloosa Paloosa"
> by C. D. Roberts (2010)

APPLE

Some experts hold that "apple" comes from the Latin *Abella*, the name of a town in the province of Campania that was renowned for its orchards and whose fruits were likely carried to the Roman frontier in England.. Subsequently it became the Old English *aeppel*, which meant "fruit" or anything round.

> An apple a day keeps the doctor away
> Apple in the morning - Doctor's warning
> Roast apple at night - starves the doctor
> outright
> Eat an apple going to bed – knock the
> doctor on the head
> Three each day, seven days a week –
> ruddy apple, ruddy cheek
> (nursery rhyme)

ARABESQUE

An ornate design of floral figures or a position in ballet, from the Italian *arabesco*, "done in the Arabic fashion," from "Arab'—originally meaning an inhabitant of Arabia. An

Arabian can refer to a breed of horse or a cartwheel-like figure skating move.

> There was a young Sicilian woman named Gina
> Who went to *Roma* to become a ballerina.
> But, alas, her flying arabesque
> Was, her teacher said, almost grotesque,
> So she shamefully skulked *homa* to Messina.

ARAUCARIA

Evergreen trees of the genus *Aracauria*, Latin for "(tree) of Araucania,." a region of central Chile, where the trees were first discovered. The species found there is popularly known as the "Monkey Puzzle Tree." Another species is the **Norfolk Island Pine**, indigenous to that South Pacific island.

> . . .the avocado, the araucaria, the orange,
> and the magnolia trees haven't lost their
> leaves, they shiver, still green, even if
> everything around them is dying.
>   Jose Donoso, *The Garden*
>   *Next Door* (1992)

ARCADIAN

Pastoral, from "Arcadia," a region of Greece often used as a setting by the bucolic poets. This should not be confused with "Acadia," an early name of Nova Scotia, the French residents of which were called "Acadians." In the mid-1800s they were exiled to south Louisiana, where they developed their own **Cajun** culture. "Cajun" comes from the word "Acadian," in the same fashion as "Injun" is a variant of "Indian."

> What dim Arcadian pastures have I
>   known
> That suddenly, out of nothing, a wind

is blown,
Lifting a veil and a darkness,
Showing a purple sea--
And under your hair the faun's eyes
Look out on me?
Alice Corbin, "What Dim
Arcadian Pastures" (1912)

ARCTIC

The area around the North Pole can be very cold indeed and so
would anyone described (figuratively, of course) as such. An
"arctic" can also mean a warm, waterproof overshoe.

Behind an ever silent façade, which
twitches uncertainly with every
expiring whim--nothing but broken
pieces, black rubbish heaps, yawning
emotional emptiness, or the cold
breath of an arctic soullessness.
E. Kretschmer, *Physique
and Character* (1921)

ARGOSY

A large merchant vessel, or a fleet of such ships. Its etymology
has spawned a few theories, but the most accepted is that it is
a corruption of the Italian *ragusea*, a ship from the Adriatic
port of Ragusa, the former name of Dubrovnik, Croatia.

Your mind is tossing on the ocean;
There where your argosies with
portly sail
Like signiors and rich burghers on
the floor,
Or as it were, the pageants of the sea,
Do overpeer the petty traffickers,
That curtsy to them, do them reverence,
As they fly by them with their woven wings.
William Shakespeare, *The
Merchant of Venice* (1598)

ARGYLE

A knitted design of solid diamond blocks contrasted in a pattern, often used for socks and sweaters. The pattern traditionally originates from the town of Argyle in Scotland.

> Bertelli was barrel-chested, white-maned,
> light on his feet, vaguely bohemian—berets,
> Argyle socks under his sandals, paisley ascots.
> Scott Spencer, *Walking the Dead*
> (1986)

ARMAGNAC

Brandy produced in the Armagnac region of France, a rival to Cognac for recognition as the best brandy in the world.

> He sipped his Armagnac, allowing each
> burning velvet sip to call in the nose
> to complicate the pleasure.
> Wyndham Lewis, *The Vulgar*
> *Streak* (1941)

ARRAS

A tapestry, from French *drap de Arras*--cloth of Arras--the French city renowned for its fifteenth-century tapestries.

> The queen's words, laced with scorn,
> pulsed through the great hall and were
> not absorbed by the beautiful Arras
> tapestries hanging from every wall.
> Jeane Westin, *The Virgin's*
> *Daughters* (2009)

ARTESIAN WELL

A well drilled through strata to reach water capable of rising to the surface by internal hydrostatic pressure, from French *(puit)*

Artesien, (well) of Artois, the region and former province of northern France where such wells were first drilled.

> There was a farmer in the dell
> Who had dug an artesian well.
> When the water gushed out
> In a furious spout,
> The farmer gave a joyful yell.

ASCOT

A type of necktie or scarf, knotted so that its wide ends lay flat upon each other. It is believed to have been popularized at Ascot, a village near Windsor, Berkshire, England, site of a famous annual horse race. It also lends its name to man's cap, also known as a **Cuffley cap,** for a Hertfordshire village.

> He was wearing, with his white duck
> trousers and blue summer-weight blazer,
> an ascot, tucked into the throat of his
> open blue oxford-cloth shirt. He looked
> in it theatrically and impossibly
> handsome like an actor hired to lounge
> by a blue pool in a glossy, expensive,
> witless magazine.
> > Anne Rivers Siddons,
> > *Homeplace* (1987)

ASHKENAZIM

Since the sixteenth century the name for the Jews of central and eastern Europe—ancestors of most American Jews. *Askhenail* is Hebrew for "Germany." Originally, *Ashkenaz* referred to an ancient land in what is now eastern Armenia.

> Medieval rabbis dubbed Germany
> *Ashkenaz,* after a passage in Jeremiah
> (51;27), and decided that after the Flood,
> one of Noah's great-grandsons, named
> Ashkenaz, had settled in Germany. I have

no idea what inspired the rabbis.
Leo Rosten, *The Joys of Yiddish*
(19680

ASSAM

A black tea named after Assam, India, where it is cultivated.

India has a great many teas.
Several are well known in the West.
But the one grown by the Assamese
Is considered by many the best.

ASTRAKHAN

The curly hide of very young lambs from the Astrakhan region of Russia on the Volga delta, from which muffs, collars and coats were made. Beginning in the late 1800s, an imitation of this fur using wool or silk with cotton has been used.

An astrakhan coat, with attached cape
and fur collar, encased her tall, noble
figure.
Annie Dillard, *The Living*
(1992)

ATTIC

The top storey under a roof, from *attic storey*. **Attic order** in classical architecture means a small, square decorative column of the type often used in a low storey above a building's main facade, a feature associated with Attica, the region around Athens. It came to mean the space enclosed by such a structure. A dry, pointed wit is sometimes referred to as **Attic wit** or **Attic salt.**

There was a fan in the attic
That kept the house cool on hot days.
For Alec was quite a fanatic

About avoiding the sun's torrid rays.

AUBUSSON

A carpet, usually of considerable size, handwoven at the villages of Aubusson and Felletin, in the *département* of Creuse in central France. Workshops were established in 1743 to manufacture pile carpets mainly for the nobility.

> Anyone with money can buy that glossy
> magazine look. You need generations
> of family history to feel comfortable
> with an Aubusson carpet that's worn on
> one corner, chintz curtains that are faded
> because they've been hanging at the
> same window for over one hundred
> years. . . .
> Shirley Conran, *Lace 2*
> (1985)

AXMINSTER

The town of Axminster in Devonshire is famous for its carpets with jute backing and soft cut-wool pile. The Axminster Carpet Factory was founded in 1755 and its carpets soon became the choice for wealthy English country homes and town houses. It is now generic for that type of carpet irrespective of where it is manufactured.

> In a moment she was bounding upstairs
> over those thick Axminster carpets—those
> awful carpets, into which her feet sank—
> down a corridor, also heavily lined with
> Axminster, past great velvet curtains,
> which seemed to stifle her as she pushed
> them aside. . . .
> L. T Meade, *Light O' the
> Morning* (1899)

AZURE

The light purplish blue color, originally found in the gemstone lazurite, can be traced back to Old French *azur* and then to the Latin *Lapis lazuli*—*lapis* ("stone") and, ultimately, Lajward, a place in Turkestan where the stone was first mined.

> I have bedimm'd
> The noontide sun, call'd forth
> > the mutinous winds,
> And 'twixt the green sea and
> > azur'd vault
> Set roaring war.
> > William Shakespeare
> > *The Tempest* (1610)

B

BACTRIAN CAMEL

The Bactrian is often confused with the dromedary camel—
the latter has a single hump and lives in hot climates, while the
former has two humps and lives in the cold mountains and
high deserts of Central Asia. Bactria, now a district of
northern Afghanistan, today is known as Balkh.

> The camel you see in the zoo
> Is a dromedary if its humps number two.
> But if there's only one
> Then it can be none
> But the Bactrian that is in view.

BADMINTON

The indoor game of shuttlecocks and rackets was thought up
one rainy day in the 1870s at Badminton House, the seat of the
Dukes of Beaufort in Gloucestershire, England. It caught on
and is now played all over the world.

> Henry and I played badminton in the yard.
> *Shuttlecock.* We loved that word. We said
> It loudly and brightly a thousand times a
> day for absolutely no reason. We'd go down
> to Woolworth's and loudly ask each other,
> "You don't think they'd have shuttlecocks
> here, do you?" The shuttlecock would go

up high in the air, its red rubber end obscene,
wonderful, and probably the only reason we
played the game. The cock would rise into
the last moment of light and then sink into
the darkness of the Pennsylvania backyard,
dropping softly onto the grass.

> A.M.. Homes, "Rockets Round
> the Moon" (1994)

BALACLAVA

Commonly called a "ski mask" in the U.S., it covers the entire
head, exposing only the eyes, and is named for the town of
Balaklava in the Russian Crimea. During the Crimean War
(1853-1856), the British army was sent knitted balaclavas to
protect against the bitterly cold weather. Nowadays it seems to
be standard issue head-gear for terrorists.

> Shortly thereafter at least 26 people
> were killed by "men clad in
> balaclavas and armed with AK47
> rifles."
>> Don Foster et al, *The
>> Theatre of Violence* (2005)

BALDACHIN

The name of this sumptuous fabric of silk and gold brocade is
the Old Italian name for Baghdad (*Baldacco*), famous in the
Middle Ages for its brocades.

> . . . in the palazzo from which the aged
> countess would stride out in a black
> baldachin-covered coach into Florence at
> noon when the gilded youth and little
> lordlings of the city went promenading
> before the exquisite stores of the Via
> Tornabuoni.
>> Sandor Marai, *Casanova in
>> Bolzano* (1940)

BALKANIZE

The division of a place or country into several small political units, often unfriendly to one another. The term comes from "Balkan Peninsula," which was partitioned into several nations in the early twentieth century. The peninsula takes its name from the Balkan Mountains in Bulgaria.

> Serbia, Herzegovina, Slovenia,
> They have all been tyrannized,
> Bosnia, Croatia, and Macedonia,
> and completely balkanized.

BALONEY

Also spelled "boloney," it is a variant of "bologna," the sausage originally from Bologna, Italy. As a term of slang it means "nonsense."

> Miss Manners expects you to treat
> others with unfailing courtesy and
> respect in all aspects of your life and
> does not want to hear any workplace
> screams of "You're full of baloney."
> Judith Martin, *Miss Manners'*
> *Guide for the Turn-of-The*
> *Millennium* (1989)

BANTAM

A breed of small fowl, extended to mean a diminutive but aggressive person. It is believed that it is native to Bantam, a town in northwestern Java, the site of the first Dutch settlement in the East Indies.

> Kartli stood spread-legged, a bantam
> fighter gazing down on the site of many
> victories. The small merchants with

their painted dolls and their charcoal-
braised cuttlefish, their burgeoning
libraries of pirated DVDs of popular
American movies looked up to him
much as a small-arms dealer will
weapons.
> Eric Van Lustbader, *The
> Testament* (2006)

BAUXITE

The general term for a rock composed of hydrated aluminum
oxides. It is the principal source of aluminum. It is named after
Les Baux, France, where it was discovered in 1821, and the
site of the first bauxite mines.

> During World War II Arkansas bauxite
> had been requisitioned for aluminum,
> furnishing more than 90% of the ore
> mined in the United States.
> Margaret Mullen, *An
> Arkansas Childhood* (1989)

BAYONET

There are two possible origins for the name. One arises from
its first appearance in the French town of Bayonne, where it
was known as a *baionnette*. The other that it is derived from
the French name for the crossbow bolt, the *bayon*.

> The municipal guard burst into a laugh
> and raised his bayonet at the child.
> Before the bayonet had touched Gavroche,
> the gun slipped from the soldier's grasp, a
> bullet had struck the municipal guardsman
> in the center of the forehead.
> Victor Hugo, *Les Misérables*
> (1862)

BEDLAM

A state of mad confusion, from St. Mary of Bethlehem, established in the thirteenth century as a priory, before being taken over by the City of London as an asylum for the mentally ill when the monasteries were dissolved in the mid-sixteenth century. It closed its doors in 1948. Over the march of years its name, shortened to "Bethlem" or "Bedlam," became synonymous with madness and chaos.

> It was bedlam on the docks, with some people trying to help the swimmers ashore, and a couple even diving in to help save some of the drowning men.
> Orson Scott Card, *The Crystal City* (2003)

BEDLINGTON

The Bedlington terrier, recognizable by its lamblike coat, top-knot, and flat head, takes it name from the mining shire of that name, in the County of Northumberland, England, where local miners had bred it for ratting.

> Even though they won't make the first move with people, Bedlington Terriers will draw curious onlookers with their unusual appearance. Those who are not very interested in dogs may even ask what kind of dog you have.
> Babette Haggerty-Brennan, *Woman's Best Friend* (2003)

BERLINE

A limousine with a glass window between the front and rear seats, from the French for "Berlin" [Germany], where it originated.

> The White Berline marks the highest
> development of the modern motor car,
> both in beauty of body design, and
> merit of chassis construction. Every
> small detail which adds to comfort,
> convenience, and safety of operations
> has been carefully and successfully
> executed.
>> Advertisement (1912)

BERMUDAS

Short pants that end at the knee. They are not uniquely Bermudian; they were created at the turn of the last century by British military forces in London—not Bermuda—by men in desk jobs whose function it was to see that personnel were appropriately dressed for duty at bases in the tropics. With their already-issued white shorts and long white stockings, the Royal Navy were probably the first to invent Bermuda shorts. They probably wore them when they founded the yacht clubs in the City of Hamilton and Town of St. George on the island of Bermuda. The island has also given the world the **Bermuda onion**, the **Bermuda Lily** and **Bermuda grass**.

> Males as a group have the fashion sense of
> cement. Oh, I realize that there are exceptions--
> men who know how to pick your elegant suits
> and perfectly color-coordinated accessories.
> But for every man walking around looking
> tasteful, there are at least ten men walking
> around wearing orange plaid Bermuda shorts
> with nonmatching boxer shorts sticking
> out above *and* below, and sometimes also
> poking out through the fly.
>> Dave Barry, *The Greatest
>> Invention in the History of
>> Mankind is Beer* (2001)

BERYL

A mineral used as a gem and the principal source for the element **beryllium.** The name is most likely derived from the ancient city of Velur (modern-day Belur) in southern India, famous for its exquisite temples.

> In the sixteenth century magicians
> prescribed beryl to be worn to win all
> debates and arguments, and yet to
> cause its bearer to be well mannered
> and amiable, and to gain understanding.
> Scott Cunningham, *Cunningham's*
> *Encyclopedia of Crystal, Gem &*
> *Metal Magic* (1988)

BIALY

The small, round yeast bread with an indentation in the center and topped with onions was a staple of the sixty-thousand Jews who lived in Bialystok, a city in northeastern Poland, before the Holocaust.

> Their eggs scrambled with dark, caramelized
> onions and lox, served with a fresh roasted
> bagel or bialy, are ethereal, and the home-team
> crowd of Upper West Siders is about as
> "genuine New York" as you can get.
> Anthony Bourdain, *The Nasty Bits*
> (2007)

BIKINI

The name for the skimpy two-piece bathing suit was coined by the French and named for the atomic bomb test of June, 1946 on the Pacific atoll of Bikini in the Marshall Islands. There is no definitive explanation for the name, though it has been suggested that it is an analogy of the explosive force of the bomb and the erotic impact of the bathing suit style on men.

> Nicola loathed bikinis, the bikini she
> regarded as the acme of vulgarity (and
> how the lines demarcated the godlike
> thorax, making polyps of the breasts. . .
> She had bought it that morning; and it
> was exceptionally vulgar, Nicola's
> bikini cutely skimpy with cutaway
> thighs, and bright white against her
> Persian flesh.
> Martin Amis, *London Fields*
> (1989)

BILBO

It has two meanings, both derive from Bilbao in the Basque country of Spain, from whence they originated: 1) a rapier-like sword; and 2) shackles on an iron bar locked to the floor, commonly used on ships. Bilboa, and not Bilbao, was, and still is, the usual spelling in English. In the Basque language the city is called Bilbo, and this is the term used by Shakespeare in referring to some iron products from Bilbao.

> It gave him airs to strut about the town,
> Flattering my lord, and railing at the
> gown,
> With brazen-hilted Bilbo to attack
> All those who dare call names behind
> his back,
> From "The Modern Poet"
> by Mary Davys (1717)

BILLINGSGATE

The kind of vulgar language once used by women vendors at the Billingsgate fish market on the River Thames, below London Bridge.

> Everybody knows that when a person
> utters low or vituperative language,
> such a person is represented as talking
> Billingsgate. The origin of this is to
> be found in the fact, that at Billingsgate
> the fish-woman are constantly abusing
> each other; and that there is a richness
> or raciness in their vituperation which
> are not to be met with in the squabbles
> and quarrels of any other class of
> persons in London.
>> James Grant, *Lights and*
>> *Shadows of London Life*
>> (1842)

BLARNEY

Flattery or misleading talk, from the Blarney stone at Blarney
Castle in Blarney, a village near Cork, Ireland. Legend has it
that anyone who kisses it receives the gift of gab.

> The servant of the mess was a very raw
> Irish lad, but recently landed; he was a
> thorough Paddy of the most amusing sort,
> full of blarney and blunder, an unceasing
> source of amusement to the young men.
>> James Fenimore Cooper, *The*
>> *Last of the Mohicans* (1862)

BOCK

Full-bodied German lager that is brewed in the fall, then aged
through winter. "Bock" is a corruption of the medieval
German town of Einbeck, located in Lower Saxony, renowned
for its six hundred-year-old brewery, believed to be the oldest
in the country.

> Johann Sebastian Bach
> Would sit beneath his cuckoo clock.
> There he would eat

And compose a new suite
While finishing off a good bock.

BOEOTIAN

A boorish, ignorant person. Boeotia was a district near Thebes in ancient Greece, the inhabitants of which were characterized by the Athenians as stupid and dull.

> I live in a market town in the North Midland
> counties, five hours from London. We are
> not wholly Boeotian. We take in the
> *Saturday Review* and the *Pall Mall Budget*.
> George Smith, "Thoughts of a
> Country Critic" (1860)

BOHEA

A black tea grown in the hills in China's northern Fukien Province. "Bohea," the name of the province in Fukien dialect. corresponds to "Wu-Shan," the name of the range where the tea is planted.

> No one has ever supped in a forecastle at
> sea, without having been struck by the
> prodigious residuum of tea-leaves, or
> cabbage stalks, in his tin-pot of bohea.
> There was no lack of material to supply
> every pipe-bowl among us.
> Herman Melville, *Redburn*
> (1849)

BOHEMIAN

The modern sense of a person with artistic interests who disregards conventional standards of behavior probably comes from the use of this Czech Republic province's name since the 15th century in France for "gypsy" (they were believed falsely to have come from Bohemia, though their first appearance in Western Europe may have been from there), or from association with Bohemian heretics. It was popularized by Henri Murger's 1845 *Scenes de la Vie de Bóheme,* the basis of Puccini's opera *La Bohème.*

> Cuckoos lead Bohemian lives,
> They fail as husbands and as wives,
> Therefore they cynically disparage
> Everybody else's marriage.
> Ogden Nash, "The Cuckoo"
> (1931)

BOKHARA

Bokhara rugs are produced in a region around the city of Lahore in Pakistan. They got their name from "Bukhara," a city in Uzbekistan, and their history dates back centuries earlier to the Turkomans who lived in the north of what is now Afghanistan.

> It was destined that I was . . . to
> purchase a Bokhara carpet, at such a
> staggering price that I felt quite
> dizzy while I was driving it home in
> the car. It was one of the best
> investments I ever made, "and if I
> were to sell it tomorrow" . . . But I
> hope I never will
> Beverley Nichols, *Laughter
> on the Stairs* (1998)

BOLIVIA

Spelled with a small "b," it is a velvet-like woolen or worsted pile fabric used for dresses. It gets its name because some of the wool is from alpacas from the Bolivian Andes.

Miss DeHaviland had a dress that was a hit.
At a party a friend asked her about the knit.
"I say, Olivia,
Is it bolivia?"
"Yes," she replied," and it looks damn good
on this Brit.

BRAZILWOOD

Sometimes called "pau-Brasil," it is a timber tree found in Brazil, used for dye. They were so numerous when the Portuguese colonized the country, they named it for them. *Brasa* in Portuguese means "burning wood," referring to the red color of the trunk of the tree, while *pau* means "wood."

> Brazil is one of the very few countries
> to receive its name from a trade good.
> Greece and Turkey, for example, never
> exported lard or fowl. Yet some
> countries and areas gave their names
> to goods. China comes immediately
> to mind. But in Brazil it was the trade
> good—the Brazilwood used for dye—
> that christened the area.
>> Kenneth Pomeranz & Steven
>> Topik, *The World that Trade
>> Created* (2006)

BREN

A type of light machine gun used by the British army in World War II. "Bren" stands for BRno-ENfield, the Czechoslovakian city where the gun was invented in 1937, and the latter, a town near London where it was redesigned and manufactured.

> He continued on, still sweeping the enemy
> positions with his Bren light machine-gun
> inflicting an extremely high number of
> casualties on the enemy, but he was killed
> by a sniper . . .

Hal D. Steward, *Recollections of
a Regimental Medical Officer*
(1983)

BRETON

A brimmed hat that rolls up all the way around, a popular shape since the end of the 19th century, originally worn by French Brittany ("Breton") peasants. A "Breton navy cap" is the peaked boatman's cap that everyone copies; the Greeks have one and so do the Poles.

> A fortune teller, who was not a gypsy or
> even Spanish but a lanky, weedy blond
> woman in a Breton hat and a faded shift . . .
> Anne Tyler, *Searching for
> Caleb* (1983)

BRIARD

This working dog's origins may be traced back to eighteenth century France. The name "Briard" came to be used in 1809 when people started calling it the *chien berger de Brie* (shepherd dog of Brie). Brie was a region in France, supposedly where this breed lived.

> What luck to find her, for once, sitting
> a record, her Briard dog, Gustave
> Flaubert, at her feet.
> May Sarton, *Mrs. Stevens
> Hears the Mermaids
> Singing* (1965)

BRITTANY

The Brittany developed in the French province of that name in the mid-1800s, quite possibly from crosses of a French spaniel with English Setters that arrived on the continent with British gentlemen hunters. The new breed was originally known as the Brittany Spaniel for its spaniel-like size and heritage, but the Brittany Club dropped "Spaniel" in 1982 to recognize this dog as the smallest of the pointers.

> "That's our newest client,
> I said.
> "It's a dog."
> "A Brittany to be precise.
> They used to call them Brittany
> Spaniels. Now they just call them
> Brittanies. They're bird dogs, origin-
> ally from the Province of Brittany.
> That's in France."
> > William G. Tapply, *A Fine
> > Line* (2002)

BROADWAY

The street in Manhattan, which originally was home to its legitimate theaters, has come to stand for the New York stage in general.

> They say the neon lights are bright
> On Broadway
> They say there's always magic in the air
> But when you're walkin' down that street
> And you ain't got enough to eat
> The glitter rubs right off and you're nowhere.
> > From "On Broadway" by
> > Mann/Weil & Lieber/Stoller

BRONZE

The name of the copper-and-tin alloy was derived from the city of Brundesium, the ancient name for Brindisi, Italy, where bronze was manufactured on a large scale.

> The bell, in unbridled frenzy, offered to
> each side of the tower in turn its bronze
> throat, emitting its tempestuous breath

which could be heard four leagues away.
Victor Hugo, *Notre-Dame de Paris* (1831)

BRUMMAGEM

The *Oxford English Dictionary* defines it as "cheap and showy or counterfeit." This came about as a result of the bad reputation gained by the forgers and false minters of Birmingham, England. The term Brummagem arose in the middle ages when the 'r' and the 'i' or 'e' in Birmingham or Bermingham were reversed in local speech.

> No novelist could have a smaller likeness to the brummagem emotion-squeezers of the Kipling type, with their playhouse fustian and their naif ethical cocksureness [than Conrad].
> H. L. Mencken, *A Book of Prefaces* (1917)

BUCKRAM

A stiff cloth, made of cotton or linen, used to cover a book or to stiffen clothes. It most likely comes from *Bukhara,* the city in central Asia from which it was imported to Europe.

> He was required to record all these things, so he found his buckram-bound record book, noted the time on the big seven-day clock, and dipped the steel nib of his pen into the ink bottle.
> Richard S. Wheeler, *Flint's Truth* (1998)

BUGGER

As a noun it can mean a homosexual male and as a verb it means to practice "buggery, that is, sodomy. It comes from

"Bulgarian" and goes back to the Middle Ages when they were regarded as heretics, and heretics were believed to be addicted to vice. In British slang it is an all-purpose expletive.

> He glanced over his shoulder at the boxes.
> "All weekend, at least. Two people. The
> bugger of it is, we'll have to list every-
> thing. Document it. Seems a bit of a pisser
> to be doing it for him, idle bugger."
> Judith Cutler, Power on Her
> Own (2003)

BUNGALOW

A small house or cottage usually having a single story. An Anglo-Indian corruption of *bangla*, an adjective which primarily means "Bengalese" or "Bengal," but which turned into a noun is the name given in India to a thatched hut.

> It was a desirable bungalow, eight-roomed
> and heavily thatched against any chance of
> leakage from rain. Under the pitch of the
> roof ran a ceiling-cloth which looked just
> as neat as a white-washed ceiling. Unless
> you knew how Indian bungalows were built
> you would never have suspected that above
> the cloth lay the dark three-cornered cavern
> of the roof, where the beams and the
> underside harboured all manner of rats,
> bats, ants, and foul things.
> Rudyard Kipling, "The Return of
> Imray" (1891)

BUNKUM

Also known as "buncombe," it is claptrap, twaddle, windy speech, especially if by a politician. In 1820 a Congressman from Buncombe County, North Carolina justified his fatuous speech before an impatient House of Representatives by declaring that he was "talking to Bunkum." The shortened version—"bunk"—is often used, which, in turn, led to the word "debunk."

> He was a diplomat, a master of bunkum,
> hokum and flattery. He was a smooth-
> talking man who could minimize the
> sound of a negative. . . .
> > Thomas W. Lippman, *Inside
> > the Mirage* (2004)

BURGUNDY

It can mean either the wine produced in the Burgundy region of France or the dark purplish color of the wine.

> A big solid cool-looking house with
> burgundy brick walls . . . .
> > Raymond Chandler, *The High
> > Window* (1942)

BURMESE

Although ancient Buddhist temples have records of a brown cat similar to today's Burmese, the modern breed is said to have been founded by a cat imported into the United States from Burma in the 1930's and then bred to a Siamese male.

> "What a love!" she exclaimed, holding
> out her hand for the cat to sniff.
> Treemonisha, a dainty sable Burmese
> that Mark had found in an alley one
> night. She examined the proffered
> fingers with aristocratic care. She
> determined that Di was appropriate
> company for Mark, and bestowed her
> approval with a tiny lick and a rub of
> her head.
> > Mercedes Lackey, *Burning
> > Water* (2005)

BYZANTINE

Characterized by intrigue and scheming as were the court politics of ancient Byzantium, the earlier name for Constantinople (present-day Istanbul, Turkey).

> Overseeing billions in trading capital, while also surviving the byzantine, often ruthless executive suite jockeying for the top job, can be a challenge for the most steeled and experienced executives . . .
>> Landon Thomas, *New York Times* (2007)

C

CAFÉ

A coffee shop or small restaurant. "Café" is French for
"coffee," which, in turn, may be toponymic; see **COFFEE**,
below.

> It's two in the mornin' on Saturday night
> At Rosalie's Good Eats Café.
> The onions are fryin', the neon is bright
> And the jukebox is startin' to play.
> And the sign on the wall says,
>   IN GOD WE TRUST,
> ALL OTHERS HAVE TO PAY.
> And it's two in the mornin' on Saturday
>   night
> At Rosalie's Good Eats Café.
>   From "Rosalie's Good Eats
>   Café" (1990) by Shel Silverstein

CAIRNGORM

A species of transparent quartz that takes its name from
Cairngorm in Inverness, Scotland, where some of the best
specimens have been found. It is often used for seals, beads,
and jewelry.

> [In Edinburgh] after dinner we walked
> out, looking at the shop-windows of

jewelers, where ornaments made of cairngorm pebbles are the most peculiar attraction. As it was our wedding day, I gave S— a golden and amethyst-bodied cairngorm beetle with a ruby head.

Nathaniel Hawthorne, ,
Passages from the English Note-Books (1870)

CALICO

The coarse cloth—usually printed with bright designs—is named after Calicut, India, the former name of Kozhikode, a seaport in the state of Kerala, where the fabric originated. The **calico cat** and **calico bass** are so named because of the colored spots on their bodies that resemble the cloth.

There was a lady from Pimlico
Who had a penchant for calico.
All who saw her agreed
That the woman indeed
Had dresses that were *magnifico.*

CALIFORNIA ROLL

This hybrid East-West fusion sushi originated in the early 1970s and is generally credited to Ichiro Manashita, of a Japanese restaurant in Los Angeles called Tokyo Kaikan. Though created for American taste, it also become popular in Japan, as *kashu-maki,* literally "California roll."

The essential sushi: begin with the pungent brocade of pressed seaweed, dry but oddly elastic, line it with a mattress of sticky rice and lay at the center, like a raw nerve cuddled in muscle, a strip of bright fish flesh— or crabmeat and avocado.

CALVADOS

The defining drink of the French region of Normandy, it is distilled from fermented apple cider and then aged two years or more in oak barrels. Its name is taken from the French *département* that produces most Calvados,

> Miguel's moods were often quite morose.
> What caused them was hard to diagnose.
> But a small dose
> Of calvados
> And his depression went *adios*.

CAMBRIC

Finely woven white linen or cotton fabric, from the Flemish textile-manufacturing city of Cambrai in northern France. The word is a combination of the city's former name in French, *Cambray*, and its Flemish name, *Kamerijk*.

> Can you make me a cambric shirt,
> Parsley, sage, rosemary, and thyme,
> Without any seam or needlework?
> And you shall be a true lover of mine.
> From "The Lover's Task"
> an old English rhyme

CAMPANILE

A detached bell tower, from the Italian *campana*, made of metal produced in Campania, a region of southern Italy on the Tyrrhenian Sea.

> A wonderful sight is that first glimpse of
> the cathedral, with the leaning campanile
> on one side and the baptistery on the other,

green turf below and a clear blue sky above!
George Eliot, *Journey to Italy* (1960)

CANADA GOOSE

It seems that when this long-necked goose, the most wide-spread breed in North America, was first spotted by Europeans who were settling what would become the United States, it was noticed that the goose was not from the local area but seemed to be flying down from the north before winter. Thus it became the "goose from Canada," or the "Canada Goose." In fact, it can found all over the continent.

> The Canada—and there are several subspecies—is probably our most recognizable goose. Often incorrectly referred to as "Canadian" geese, these birds and their Vs in the sky are a herald of autumn and spring as they pass overhead.
> Steve Smith, *Hunting Ducks and Geese* (2003)

CANARY

The yellow song-bird is a native of the Canary Islands, hence the name—not the other way around; in fact, the island derives its name from the Latin for "Isle of the Dogs," because of the native canine population there. "Canary" is also a popular shade of yellow and a type of natural diamond.

> Tweetee was a canary bird
> Who could sing like you've never heard.
> No ditties warbled he,
> But a full symphony!
> His favorite was Beethoven's Third.

CANOPY

A cloth covering held horizontally above a person or an object for protection, from the ancient city of Canopus, Egypt, about fifteen miles east of Alexandria, where it probably originated.

> There are multiple layers to penetrate
> —clouds, tree canopy, lower-level flora.
> There's just no way around it: almost
> anything could be hiding in the rain
> forest.
> > Michael Crichton, *The Lost
> > World* (1996)

CANTALOUPE

The popular melon was named after the commune Cantalupo in the Sabine Hills near Tivoli, Italy, a summer residence of the Pope, where it was originally cultivated around 1700 from seeds brought from Armenia.

> I remember Sylvie saying that she had
> learned from us to put salt on her
> cantaloupe. I don't know where that
> comes from. Mother did it, we always
> did it. It makes it taste sweeter.
> > Beth Gutcheon, *Good-Bye and
> > Amen* (2009)

CANTER

With respect to horses, a canter is a "three beat" gait, between a trot and a gallop. It is sometimes called a "lope." When English pilgrims traveled to Canterbury the easy gait at which they rode was described as a "Canterbury gallop." Over time this was shortened to "Canterbury" and finally to "canter" used both as noun and verb.

> I don't know any more beautiful

> music than the beat of a cantering
> horse's hoofs on a crisp moonlit night,
> and Lady had one of the smoothest
> gaits of any horse that ever ran.
>> Ralph Moody, *The Home*
>> *Ranch* (1994)

CAPE COD

The Cape Cod house style originated in colonial New England. Today, the term refers to Cape Cod-shaped houses popular during the 1930s, 1940s, and 1950s. The stormy weather of Massachusetts' Cape Cod region inspired the style.

> In America one of the earliest typical
> houses was the "Cape Cod Cottage,"
> built around a single chimney with
> one or two sleeping rooms on the
> ground floor for the benefit of the
> mother who generally did the cook-
> ing as well as cared for the children
>> Frank A. Bourne, "The
>> Workingman's Home"
>> (1914)

CAPESKIN

The leather of the South African sheep takes its name from the Cape of Good Hope, where they graze on the veldts. The skin is strong and durable and often used to make lightweight dress gloves.

> In this hotel lobby, pull on my black
> capeskin gloves. Slide a hand into
> the crimson silk. Tighten my fist on
> the grip of my bag. Go slowly down
> these steps.
>> J. P. Donleavy, *The Beastly*
>> *Beatitudes of Balthazar B*
>> (1968)

CAPITOL

The name of the building where Congress meets comes from the Latin. *Capitolium,* the temple of Jupiter Optimus Maximus on the Capitoline Hill in ancient Rome. With a small "c" it means the building which a state legislature meets.

> I often confuse *capitol*
> With its homonym *capital.*
> I have an inkling
> The first's a building
> And the latter governmental.

CAPRIS

Short pants that extend to mid-calf, not to be confused with Bermuda shorts which end at the knee. Sometimes called "clam diggers" or "pedal pushers," they were first popular in the late 1950s and early 1960s. The name comes from the Italian island of Capri, a popular holiday resort, where they were popular during that time.

> She was wearing capris, which emphasized
> legs that went from here to China . . .
>   Elizabeth George, *This Body of Death* (2010)

CARDIGAN

A sweater that buttons or zips down the front was named after James Brudenell, the seventh Earl of Cardigan, the English general during the Crimean War who led the charge of the Light Brigade and favored such a sweater. So it is both an eponym and a toponym, Cardigan being a town in Wales for which his inherited earldom was named.

He dressed like a math teacher, or like
Mr. Rogers, in cardigan sweaters and
canvas sneakers, and he had a crew cut.
Elin Hilderbrand, *Nantucket
Nights* (2003)

CASABA

A type of winter melon, its name comes from *kasaba*, the former name of Turgutlu, Turkey. Also a colloquial synonym for breasts, along the line of maracas or hooters.

The view he had down the front of her
Shirt—wow, casabas like that deserved
a lot of attention and he was willing to
dedicate himself to them.
Stella Cameron, *Glass Houses* (2001)

CASHMERE

Old spelling of Kashmir, the Himalayan kingdom where fine, downy wool was obtained from long-haired goats found there in abundance, and famous for woolen clothing during the British Raj.

Men first began craving cashmere in
1937, when Lana Turner wore her tight
cashmere sweater in the film *They Won't
Forget*. And nobody did forget that sweater.
From that moment, women began their
cashmere collections.
Nina Garcia, *The One Hundred*
(2008)

CATACOMBS

A series of underground chambers with recesses for graves. The catacombs of San Sebastiano in Rome are the first to be called "catacombs"—*catacumbas* in Latin. What is not clear is if the word is derived from the place itself or the cemetery.

> We were in a basement jazz club that
> looked like a catacomb, and sat at a bar
> tended by a thin man who looked like a
> corpse taking advantage of the short
> commute.
>> Elizabeth McCracken, *Niagara*
>> *Falls All Over Again* (2002)

CAUCASIAN

A member of the Caucasoid ethnic division of humankind having certain physical characteristics such as skin color (from very light to brown), and fine hair ranging from straight to wavy or curly. It is named after the Caucasus region, from an old belief that the "Aryan" race originated there.

> His hair was not age-white but only
> extremely blond, as if he were a
> natural albino who had elected to have
> re-pigmentation treatment limited to his
> eyes, which were a very pale blue, and
> his skin, of an untanned Caucasian pallor.
>> Fred Saberhagen, *Berserker Man*
>> (1984)

CEDAR OF LEBANON

The tall evergreen tree, often mentioned in Scripture, is native to Lebanon, Syria, and Turkey and appears, in a stylized version, on the Lebanese flag.

> These magnificent cedars grew plentifully
> on the mountain slopes of Lebanon in
> Solomon's time and were held in high
> esteem not only for their beauty and
> delightful fragrance, but also for the
> durability of the reddish-colored wood.

Wilma R. James, *Gardening
with Biblical Plants* (1983)

CHAMBRAY

A plain woven fabric with colored warp and white fillings,
giving it a mottled appearance. It is used for shirts, children's
clothes, dresses, etc. It is an alternative spelling of *Cambrai*,
the city in France where the cloth was originally made.

> Looking straight ahead gave her a
> great view of how broad his chest
> was in his chambray shirt. The shirt
> looked soft from washing, and
> Maddie restrained herself from
> reaching out and touching it. That
> was the kind of thing that men often
> misconstrued.
> > Jennifer Crusie, *Tell Me
> > Lies* (2004)

CHAMPAGNE

The bubbly wine is named for France's northernmost wine-
gproducing area, about ninety miles northeast of Paris, where
it was first developed.

> I get no kick from champagne,
> Mere alcohol doesn't thrill me at all,
> So tell me why should it be true,
> That I get a kick out of you?
> > Cole Porter, from "I Get
> > a Kick Out of You."

CHANTILLY LACE

A finely decorative floral lace sewn onto a sheer hexagonal
mesh ground, it is named for the French town of Chantilly,

famous for it's production. "Chantilly" also refers to a kind of porcelain made there, as well as a sweet whipped cream.

> Chantilly lace and a pretty face
> And a pony tail hanging down,
> That wiggle in the walk and giggle
> in the talk
> Makes the world go round.
> Chorus of "Chantilly Lace" (1958)
> pop hit by the Big Bopper

CHARLATAN

Someone who claims to have a skill that he or she does not have. It is a variant of the Italian *cerretano*, meaning a resident of the Italian town of Cerreto, in Umbria, from where some of the first mountebanks or "quacks" came.

> He tries hard to summarize the theories
> of the French psychoanalyst Jacques
> Lacan (1901-81) . . . but duly observes
> that Lacan has his detractors. "Noam
> Chomsky is reputed to have dismissed
> him as an 'amusing and perfectly self
> -conscious charlatan.' "
> Kent Owen, *Wall Street Journal*
> (2008)

CHARLESTON

The fast dance associated with the 1920s is named for Charleston, South Carolina. It became popular when the song of the same name by James P. Johnson debuted in 1923. The dance had been performed a couple of decades earlier by African-Americans in the Charleston area.

> Charleston! Charleston
> Made in Carolina.
> Some dance, some prance,
> I'll say.

There's nothing finer than the
Charleston, the Charleston.

> From "Charleston" (1923)
> Lyrics by Cecil Mack

CHARTREUSE

A greenish yellow color, so named because of its similarity to the French liqueur of that name made by the Carthusian monks at *la Grande Chartreuse*, their monastery, near Grenoble, which is named after the nearby Chartreuse Mountains.

> Her frosted, wet-looking lipstick
> seemed less than businesslike, but it
> suited her, as did the chartreuse suit
> that hugged her contours a little more
> snugly than was strictly necessary.
>
> > Robert Ludlum, *The Janson Directive* (2002)

CHERRY

The origin of the name of the tree and its fruit is unclear, though most agree it comes from the Greek *kerasos*. It may have been named for the city of that name in the ancient province of Pontus in Asia Minor, though some etymologists claim that the reverse is more likely.

> Cherries of the night are riper
>   Than the cherries pluckt at noon
> Gather to your fairy piper
>   When he pipes his magic tune:
> > Merry, merry,
> > Take a cherry;
> > Mine are sounder,
> > Mine are rounder,
> > Mine are sweeter
> > For the eater
> > Under the moon
> And you'll be fairies soon.

CHESTERFIELD

Both a kind of couch and a style of overcoat, named for the fourth Earl of Chesterfield, Philip Dormer Stanhope (1694-1773, a politician and writer, known for his gracious living and his letters to his son. Chesterfield is in Derbyshire and the Earldom was made a title in the English peerage in 1616.

> It had black and primrose walls lined
> with rare editions, deep chairs, and a
> Chesterfield sofa suggesting the
> embraces of the houris, a black baby
> grand, a wood fire in an old-fashioned
> hearth and Sevres vases filled with
> flowers of the season. . . .
>> Dorothy Sayers, *Whose
>> Body?* (1923)

CHESTNUT

The chestnut tree is of the genus *Castanea*, derived from the Greek, *kastaneia,* believed to mean either "nut from Castana," referring to a city in central Greece, or "nut from Castanaia," a city of Pontus, a region of the Black Sea in what is today Turkey. However, it might just be that both places take their names from the trees, not the other way around.

> Under a spreading chestnut tree
> The village smithy stands;
> The smith, a mighty man is he,
> With large and sinewy hands:
> And the muscles of his brawny arms
> Are strong as iron bands.
>> Henry W. Longfellow,
>> from "The Village Smithy"

CHEVIOT

A wool fabric that comes from the hornless sheep of the Cheviot hills on the England/Scotland border. It is also the name of the sheep breed itself.

> I think that my cheviot suit, the ham
> I was eating among the hungry and
> ragged, and my elegance were a desire
> to stand apart from all that . . . .
> Aleksander Wat, *My Century*
> (1988)

CHINA

Good ceramic ware, originally imported from China to Europe in the sixteenth century. A style in art and craft reflecting Chinese influence is called **chinoiserie**, the French term for "Chinese." **Crepe de chine** ("crepe of China") is a silk crepe often used in women's blouses and dresses.

> Not louder shrieks to pitying heaven are cast,
> When husbands, and when lapdogs breathe
> their last;
> Or when rich china vessels fallen from high,
> In glittering dust and painted fragments lie!
> Alexander Pope, from "The Rape
> of the Lock" (1712)

CHIHUAHUA

The diminutive short-haired dog hails from Chihuahua, Mexico's largest state.

> He's a mutt with mostly Chihuahua blood,
> which meant he's small enough to be one
> of my body parts like a heart or liver with
> little ears and a tail.
> Jack Gantos, *What Would Joey
> Do?* (2004)

CHRISTIANA

A ski turn in which the skier swings his body from a crouch to change direction or to stop. Commonly shortened to "Christy," it is named for Christiana, the former name for Oslo, Norway.

> The snow was blue-green through the
> colored lenses of her glasses. As she caught
> up with Jacques, she braked sharply, going
> into a Christy which raised a white powder
> spray all around her.
> Henri Troyat, *The Seed and
> the Fruit* (1956)

CILICE

It traditionally refers to a hairshirt, an undergarment made of animal hair. It comes from the Latin *Cilicium*, a covering made of goats' hair from Cilicia, a Roman province in Asia Minor. It was adopted by zealous Christians as a form of corporal mortification. The modern cilice is a chain that is worn around the thigh, chafing and pricking the user's skin.

> We also discussed my spirit of sacrifice, of
> mortification, and the practice of flagellation.
> Guadelupe gave me my first cilice, rather,
> she sold it to me, since the "non-giving
> apostolate" is customary in Opus Dei.
> Maria Del Carmen Tapia, *Beyond
> the Threshold: A Life in Opus Dei*
> (1997)

CLYDESDALE

The big draft horses—famous for drawing big Budweiser beer wagons—come from the Clyde River valley of Scotland.

> I liked seeing the beer wagons with their

big Percheron or Clydesdale teams, and
liked watching the fancy carriages with
their fine driving horses all neck-reined
up and prancing along.

> Louis L'Amour, *To Tame A
> Land* (1955)

COACH

A large, closed, four-wheeled carriage with an elevated
exterior seat for the driver; a stagecoach. It was named after
Kocs, a town in Hungary where they were first made.

> "Still," said Lucy Pippin hesitantly, "it
> would be nice to live in the big house, and
> to have a coach and four, and to be able to
> travel to London for the season, and to
> Bath to take the waters, or to Brighton for
> the sea-bathing . . . .

> Neil Gaiman, *Stardust* (2000)

COFFEE

The word entered English in 1598 via Italian *caffè*, via Turkish
kahve, from Arabic *qahwa*. Its ultimate origin is uncertain,
there being several legendary accounts of the genesis of the
drink. One possible origin is the Kaffa region in Ethiopia,
where the plant originated (its native name there being *bunna*).
Coffee beans were first exported from Ethiopia to Yemen.

> I'm feelin' mighty lonesome
> Haven't slept a wink
> I walk the floor from nine to four
> In between I drink
> Black coffee
> Love's a hand-me-down brew
> Never knew a Sunday
> In this weekend room.

> from "Black Coffee" (a
> song by Burke & Webster)

COGNAC

A grape brandy from the Cognac district of France.

> Carl and Claire were fond of cognac brandy,
> But it quickly made Claire quite randy.
> After just one small snifter
> In his arms Carl would lift her
> And dash to whatever room was handy.

COLOGNE

Cologne water (*eau de Cologne*) is a light perfume first concocted in the German city of Cologne where it is called *Kölnischwasser*, Köln being the German name for Cologne.

> Behind him was the Maresciallo,
> pompous and important, rubbing his
> smooth red face. He was the only man
> in Montelepre who had himself shaved
> every day. Even on the platform Guiliano
> could smell the strong cologne with which
> the barber had showered him.
> > Mario Puzo, *The Sicilian* (1984)

CONGA

The name of the line dance and the drums come from "Congo," the region of central Africa that saddles the Congo River. In the late 1930s Desi Arnaz, remembering carnival in Cuba when people in the streets would dance in *la conga* lines, started a conga craze in the United States. Drummers who played *la conga* rhythms at carnival, were called *gongueros* and their instruments *tambores de conga*, translated as **conga drums**.

> A wall of music stormed up from
> the bandstand. Powerful rhythms

from the conga drums started instant-
aneous gyrations in the dancers' hips.
The conga line formed haphazardly
but soon subjected itself to the kicking,
hip-jerking discipline of the festive
dance. The dancers screamed "One,
two, three, la conga!!" over and over, as
if they had never been or ever would be
happier than they were at this moment.
Rick DeMarinis, *The Year of
the Zinc Penny* (1989)

COPPER

The metallic element's name comes from the Latin *cuprum,* a
contraction of *Cyprium,* meaning "Cyprian (metal)," after the
Greek *Kyprios* for the Mediterranean island of Cyprus, where
copper was mined. It is also refers to the metal's reddish-
brown color.

Below is . . . a broad clear pond,
sparkling like burnished copper
in the sunlight.
Nikolai Gogol, *Dead
Souls* (1842)

CORDOVAN

A type of leather manufactured originally at Cordoba in the
Andalusia region of Spain. *Cordoban* means "from Cordoba"
in Spanish.

The night on which they were packing one
of Fernanda's bridal trunks, the things
were so well organized that the schoolgirl
knew by heart which were the suits and
cloth slippers she would wear crossing
the Atlantic and the blue cloth coat with
copper buttons and the cordovan shoes
she would wear when she landed.

Gabriel García Márquez, *One Hundred Years of Solitude* (1967)

CORINTHIAN

A luxury-loving person, profligate, man-about-town. For the expensive living standards that prevailed in the Ancient Greek city of Corinth. It was renowned for the temple prostitutes of Aphrodite, the goddess of love, who served the wealthy merchants and the powerful officials living in or traveling in and out of the city. The **Corinthian order** is the most ornate of the classical orders of architecture.

> He was a very notable Corinthian. From his wind-swept hair (most difficult to achieve), to the toes of his gleaming Hessians, he might have posed as an advertisement for the Man of Fashion.
> Georgette Heyer, *The Corinthian* (1940)

COTON DE TULEAR

A type of Bichon. A descendant, the Bichon Tenerife (now extinct), was introduced to the Indian Ocean islands of Mauritius and Reunion by sailors in the sixteenth century. It acquired a long, cotton-like coat and was known as the Coton de Reunion. It is now extinct, but its descendant, the Coton de Tulear, appeared at the pirate and slave-trading port of Tulear, Madagascar, during the seventeenth century. Adopted by the ruling Merina tribal monarchy, it quickly became known as "The Royal Dog of Madagascar."

> The Coton de Tulear is another gorgeous dog. Don't let their delicate appearance fool you; they are filled with spunk and

personality. . . . They look like prima
donnas, but they have a lot to say.
>   Babette Haggerty-Brennan,
>   *Woman's Best Friend*
>   (2003)

CRAVAT

A kind of scarf, from "Cravate," a Croatian, from Serbo-
Croatian *hrvat*, a Croat. The neckband was worn by Croatian
mercenaries in the service of France.

> Unlike the dandies, Chopin preferred
> muted cravats A former pupil recalled
> that in daytime Fryderyk wore "a long
> and wide cravat, covering his shirt"
> and a broad white silk cravat when he
> performed in formal surroundings. To
> tie a cravat was an art, and, according
> to *L'Arte de la toilette*, a book then in
> wide circulation, there were seventy-
> two ways of doing it.
>   Tad Szulc, *Chopin in Paris*
>   (1999)

CREMONA

A violin made by one of the great violin craftsmen of
Cremona, Italy, from the sixteenth to the eighteenth century,
such as Stradivari, Guarnieri, or one of the Amati family.
Cremona nestles on the Po river, fifty miles southeast of
Milan.

> There can be little doubt that the old
> Cremonas or Amatis owe their
> nature to the antiquity of the wood of
> which they were made, than to any
> secret peculiarity in their construction.
>   Ebenezer Brewer, *Sound*
>   *and its Phenomena* (1864)

CRETIC

A trisyllabic metrical foot having an unaccented or short syllable between two accented or long syllables. Used in ancient poetry, it is also called "amphimacer." It literally mean "from Crete."

> The poet was in no way averse
> To using the cretic in his verse.
> The problem was
> The poet does
> Prefer his syllables to be terse.

CRETONNE

Originally a hemp and linen weave material from the town of Creton in Normandy, France. In the 1920s it had become fashionable as a medium weight cotton furniture fabric.

> She sat by the window watching the
> evening invade the avenue. her head
> was leaned against the window curtains
> and in her nostrils was the odour of
> dusty cretonne. She was tired.
> > James Joyce, "Eveline,"
> > *Dubliners* (1914)

CUBAN HEELS

A high, straight heel, without the curve of the "French" or "Louis XV" heel. In the 1860s many men wore the high heels which were then called "Cuban Heels" or "Spanish Heels." Cuba's place in the etymology of the name is unknown.

> The birth of the Mods probably took
> place in London and the Southeast.
> The boys dressed in well cut suits with
> tight trousers and wobbled about on

boots with Cuban heels and pointed
toes. The Cuban was a popular shoe
with the shorties too, until they realized
all the boys had reached for the sky as
well, adding three inches to their height.
Andrew Cosway, *Green Apples
& Armagnac* (2006)

CURRANT

The little fruit derives its name from "Corinth," the region of
ancient Greece occupying most of the Isthmus of Corinth and
part of the northeastern Peloponnesus.

Shall I give you white currants?
I do not know why, but I have a
sudden fancy for this fruit.
At the moment, the idea of them
cherishes my senses,
And they seem more desirable than
flawless emeralds.
Amy Lowell, from "White
Currents" (1925)

CYNICAL

This word, with its roots in the Greek philosophical school
(Cynics), has several shades of meaning, including, according
to *Webster*, "contemptuously distrustful of human nature and
motives." "Cynic" is derived from the first part of *Kunosarge*,
the gymnasium just outside Athens where the founder of the
Cynics taught.

Thackeray's (superficially) cynical outlook
on life must have irritated Dickens, whose
boisterous, unashamed enjoyment of all
good things could never have been
understandable to the other.
J.W.T. Ley, *The Dickens Circle*
(1919)

D

DAIQUIRI

The cocktail made of rum, lime juice, and sugar was originally concocted at Daiquiri beach, near Havana, Cuba.

> Gregorio brought *Pilar* to one of the Havana docks early that evening but, busy drinking daiquiris and dining at the Floridita, and winding up landlubber connections as though we would be gone for a year . .
> Mary Welsh Hemingway, *How It Was* (1976)

DALMATIAN

Known for it's fire station duties, and made famous by the book and film *101 Dalmatians*, these dogs are thought to have originated in Northern India, where they were used as sentries. The breed traveled to Dalmatia, a region of Croatia located along the Adriatic Sea, during the sixteenth century and has since become popular in Europe and America.

> The Dalmatian's development has been primarily in England where the breed was exceptionally popular as a carriage dog during the Regency period.
> Juliette Cunliffe, *The Encyclopedia of Dog Breeds* (2003)

DALMATIC

An ecclesiastical garment worn during certain Roman Catholic services. It has wide sleeves, is open at the sides, and is often embroidered. From Latin *dalmatica vestis* ("Dalmatian garment"), because originally made of white wool from Dalmatia, Croatia.

> He loved to kneel down on the cold marble pavement, and watch the priest, in his stiff flowered dalmatic, slowly and with white hands moving aside the veil of the tabernacle, or raising aloft the jewelled lantern-shaped monstrance with that pallid wafer . . . .
>> Oscar Wilde, *The Picture of Dorian Gray* (1890)

DAMASK

A very old type of figured fabric, first made of silk from *Damascus,* the Syrian city famous in medieval times for its silk production,

> As they ate, he admired the table with its white damask cloth, blue Limoges china, and slender vase with one blue iris.
>> "Good taste," he told Peter . . . .
>> Judith Michael, *Private Affairs* (1987)

DANISH

Informal name for Danish pastry, the sugary concoctions which were reputedly first made in Denmark.

> He walked in the direction of the Civic Center and stopped at the Foster's on the corner of Geary and Van Ness for Danish and coffee.
>> Robert Stone, *Dog Soldiers* (1974)

DEMERARA

A variety of unrefined brown sugar, long popular in Europe, and recently available in the United States. It is named for a region of Guyana by the Demerara River. Today, the bulk of its production is on the Indian Ocean island of Mauritius.

> Most demerara sugar available is made from refined white sugar with molasses added. (To find the genuine stuff, look on the packet: there should be no list of ingredients as demerara sugar is just that, not sugar and molasses).
> Anthony Telford, *The Kitchen Hand* (2003)

DENIM

The fabric of "blue jeans" is believed to be a contraction of the French term *serge de Nimes,* as the material originated in that city of southern France.

> An appealing fabric for courtship worn by men and women around the world is blue denim. As denim cloth fades it takes on the mood and elevating pastel hues of a clear blue sky. . . Highly diluted by white, faded denim evokes amicable feelings in viewers and makes it easier for them to approach. . . .
> David B. Givens, *Love Signals.* (2005)

DENVER BOOT

The infamous wheel clamp got its popular name from Denver, Colorado, the city where it was invented in 1953 and first used.

> Denver Boots and omelets: is that all
> this city is famous for? We've got the
> Denver Boot in San Francisco. We
> thought we were supposed to eat it.
> In fact, The Denver Boot and the
> Denver omelet taste quite a bit alike.
>> Herb Caen, from speech
>> before the Denver Press
>> Club (1996)

DERBY

Americans started calling the bowler hat a derby when the Earl of Derby wore one to the Derby horse race held annually at Epsom Downs in Surrey, England. It was founded in 1780 by Edward Smith-Stanley (1752-1834), the twelfth Earl of Derby. Derby (or Derbyshire) is a county in Central England. A "derby" also refers to any formal race with a more or less open field of contestants, such as a soapbox derby.

> I thought I would dress in baggy pants,
> big shoes, a cane and a derby hat. everything
> a contradiction: the pants baggy, the coat
> tight, the hat small and the shoes large.
>> Charlie Chaplin

DOLLAR

The basic money unit used in the United States and several other countries. It comes from the German *Taler*, short for *Joachimsthaler*, a coin made from silver mined from the thal (valley) of Joachimsthal, a town in the Erzgeirge Mountains of the Czech Republic.

> The dollar has been called spondulicks,
> bucks, dough, wad, ready, boodle,
> beans, and simoleon, which is perhaps
> done to make it more acceptable: call

it money and it's serious.
Jason Goodwin, *Greenback* (2003)

DONNYBROOK

This word for a drunken brawl is named for a suburb of Dublin, Ireland. Since medieval times its annual fair was notorious not only for its drinking but also for the brawls that would break out. They became so predictable they had to shut the fair down in 1855 In 1822, a typical fair day's complaints were "for broken heads, black eyes, bloody noses, squeezed hats, singed, cut and torn inexpressibles, jocks and upper benjamins, loodies, frocks, tippets, reels and damaged leghorns, together with sundry assaults, fibbings, cross buttocks, and ground floorings too numerous to mention."

> The Sabres responded by putting several enforcers on the ice, starting a donnybrook that resulted in 100 minutes in penalties, 63 of them assessed against Buffalo, and a $10,000 fine for Buffalo.
> Jeff Z. Klein and Karl-Eric Reif, *New York Times* (2007)

DOWNING STREET

Because certain official residences and offices are located on London's Downing Street, it is treated by the media as the personification of the British government.

> The language of *The World at One* is clearly not that of *the Times*. . . . [T]here is an element of simplification, even personification, in "Downing Street says . . ." where a quality newspaper would be likely to identify a government spokesperson.

Andrew Crisell, *Understanding Radio* (1994)

DUFFEL

Sometimes spelled "duffle," it is a type of cloth that was originally sold in the town of Duffel, in Belgium. In the United States it is usually part of "duffel bag," which in the United Kingdom. is referred to as a "holdall."

> A sailor carrying his big duffel
> Went into a bar and got into a scuffle.
> Somebody grabbed his dog tag,
> So he hit him with his bag
> And the fight turned into a kerfuffle

DUM-DUM

A bullet developed by the British for use in India—at the Dum-Dum Arsenal—on the North West Frontier in the late 1890s. It is a jacketed .303 bullet with the jacket nose open to expose its lead core. The phrase 'dum-dum' was later taken to include any soft-nosed or hollow pointed bullet. The Hague Convent- ion of 1899 outlawed its use during warfare.

> Sometimes the Chinese--the Marines as
> well--used a pocketknife or bayonet to
> gouge a deep cross into the soft lead
> point of a bullet so that when it hit a
> man it splayed out, creating a much
> broader wound. Dum-dum bullets, they
> were called. They were supposed to be
> illegal, Geneva Convention rules, but
> everyone used them, both sides.
> James Brady, *The Marines of
> Autumn: A Novel of the
> Korean War* (2000)

DUNGAREES

The etymology of the word used to identify heavy cotton pants (such as overalls) goes back to a thick cloth, *Dongari Kapar*, which was offered for sale in next to the Dongari Killa, the fort of what was then known as Bombay. Dyed in indigo, the traditional blue cloth was used by Portuguese sailors and cut wide so that the legs could be quickly rolled up when required.

> Sailors passed, yellow powerful
> Scandinavian and dark men with
> earrings from southern latitudes,
> in red or checked shirts, blue
> dungarees and glazed black hats
> with trailing ribbons, or in cheap
> and clumsy shore clothes.
> > Joseph Hergesheimer,
> > *Java Head* (1918)

DUTCH

There are several slang meanings of "Dutch." One is anger or temper; another—"in Dutch"—means to be in trouble; yet another, is that each person pays his own way, as in "Dutch treat" or "going Dutch."

> Pookie always paid for the hot chocolate;
> it was understood to be her treat. In fact,
> many places we went, whether out to
> dinner, to dance, or to drink, she often
> insisted we at least go dutch.
> > John Nichols, *The Sterile
> > Cuckoo* (1965)

E

EBOLA

The lethal virus takes its name from the Ebola River Valley in the Congo (the former Zaire) where the first case was detected in 1976. A close relative is the **Marburg virus**, first reported in 1967 when lab workers in Marburg, Germany contracted it while processing kidneys from infected green monkeys obtained from Uganda. Other toponymous viruses are **Hantavirus** (derived from the Hantan River in Korea); **Norwalk virus** (first identified in 1972 in Norwalk, Ohio and also known as Norovirus); **Ross River virus** (from the Ross River in Queensland, Australia); and **West Nile virus** (first identified in the West Nile District of Uganda in 1937)

> She had no potential husband in tow. Her only current suitor was Harvey Beerbaum whom she rated just ahead of the Ebola virus.
> Parnell Hall, *Dead Man's Puzzle* (2009)

ENGLISH

The spin given to a ball (as in billiards or pool). by striking it on one side or releasing it with a sharp twist, from the French "Angle" (angled), which being similar to "Anglais," (French for "English") led to confusion between the two words. There are many "English" toponyms, including "English horn," "English muffin," and "English saddle."

> Nor did Robber like best to put English
> on an otherwise limp return and leave
> some graceful athlete splayed belly down
> on the table while the little plastic sphere
> went click, click clicking off into a dusty
> corner.
>
> Meredith Sue Willis, *Dwight's
> House and Other Stories*
> (2004)

EPSOM SALT

One of the earliest findings of magnesium sulfate, the scientific name of Epsom salt, occurred in the 1500s in Epsom, England, which explains the first half of the name.

> When Fidelis prepared himself for sleep
> by listening to the radio and then soaking
> his feet in a hot Epsom salt bath that she
> prepared for him after he drank his first
> highball.
>
> Louise Erdrich, *The Master
> Butchers Singing Club* (2003)

ERMINE

The weasely little critter with the valuable white fur traces its name to the Medieval Latin *mus Armenius*—"Armenian mouse."

> Despite the heat, the good lady had put
> on a jet-black mantelet resembling a dalmatic,
> on top of which there hung an ermine stole,
> the wearing of which seemed to relate not to
> the temperature or the season, but to the
> nature of the ceremony.
>
> Marcel Proust, *Sodom and
> Gomorrah* (1921)

F

FAIENCE

A kind of majolica pottery, typically embellished with colorful glazes. The name is short for *(vaiselle de) Faience*, "(vessel of) Faenza," a northern Italian town that was a leading center of majolica production during the Renaissance. In France, "faience" is used for all glazed earthenware, and corresponds nearly to the English word "crockery."

> Helen cast a listless look into a
> window where here were some
> jars of limoges and plates of
> modern majolica. She asked him
> the price of some of the faience.
> It seemed very little, and he
> explained that it was merely
> earthenware painted in imitation
> of the faience.
> William Dean Howells,
> *A Woman's Reason* (1882)

FEZ

The red felt cap without a brim worn by men in Turkey, Egypt, Indonesia, and some North African countries traces its name from the city of Fez in Morocco where they were made.

> Meanwhile Burroughs and I also got some
> opium from a guy in a red fez in the Zoco
> Chico and made some home made pipes
> with old olive oil cans and smoked

singing "Willie the Moocher" . . .
> Jack Kerouac, *Lonesome*
> *Traveler* (1989)

FIACRE

A coach for hire, so named because they were first hired out
from Hotel de St. Fiacre in Paris in the seventeenth century.

> At the Rue Guénégaud she called a fiacre,
> and directed him to drive to the Rue de
> Harlay . . . . The fiacre crossed the Pont-
> Neuf and entered the Rue de Harlay by the
> Place Dauphine; the driver was paid as
> the door opened . . .
> > Alexandre Dumas, *The Count of*
> > *Monte Cristo* (1845)

FLAMENCO

The origin of the name of the Spanish musical form is elusive.
As it means "from Flanders" in Spanish, some attribute it to
the early 1500s and the Flemish courtiers during the reign of
Charles V. Their bright clothing inspired the names given
things garish, such as flamingos and Flamenco. Others say
Flamenco—still referring to the Flemish—was the nationality
erroneously given by the common people to Gypsies.

> My grandmother used to refer to Spanish
> flamenco dancing as "Spanish flamingo
> dancing," which, as a child, I found hilarious,
> but a it turns out she wasn't so far off the
> mark—flamingo and flamenco share the same
> root, being associated with the Latin *flamma*,
> meaning "flame"; The dancers were thought
> to take on the same ruddy complexion as
> that attributed to the Flemish.
> > Andrea Barham, *The Pedant's*
> > *Return* (2007)

FLEET STREET

English journalism, from the name of the street of central London along which many newspaper publishers are located.

> It's still hard to improve on "Scoop,"
> Evelyn Waugh's 1938 satire of accident-
> prone, irresponsible Fleet Street hacks
> covering wars no one cares about . . .
> > Alan Riding, *New York Times* (2006)

FLORENTINE

This is not only the name of a citizen of Florence, Italy, but, as well, a classic Christmas cookie from Tuscany. In 1533 Catherine d'Medici became queen of France; she so loved spinach that she insisted it be served at every meal; to this day, dishes made with spinach are known as "Florentine" because Catherine had come from Florence.

> *I wonder if there's spinach in my teeth,*
> Paige was thinking as she polished off
> the last of her eggs Florentine. *God, I*
> *hope not.*
> > Elizabeth Lenhard, *Date with*
> > *Death* (2002)

FRANK

Straightforward or outspoken, from Latin *Francus*The Franks were one of the Germanic tribes that conquered Celtic Gaul in the early Christian era. They called it "France," country of the Franks. The connection is that only Franks, as the conquering class, had the status of "freemen."

> "I will be perfectly frank," she promised,
> with an uneasy condition that she had not
> been frank with him and with a doubt if

she could be quite frank with him the next
time.

Jack London, *Martin Eden*
(1909)

FRENCH

The verb "to french" is a culinary term meaning to cut into
thin strips before cooking, a method originated by French
cooks. **Frenchify** means to give something a French quality or
to assume Gallic ways. Among the numerous "French"
toponyms are "French bulldog," French window," and
"French toast."

> This defiance had inspired a bizarre but
> much-reported campaign to 'de-Frenchify'
> America, including the renaming of 'french
> fries' as 'freedom fries.' Bill O'Reilly of
> Fox News, one of the most exuberant of
> the media hawks, simply told his audience,
> 'Don't buy French stuff': the French were
> now just 'weasels.'
>
> Paul Rutherford, *Weapons of Mass
> Persuasion: Marketing the War
> Against Iraq* (2004)

FRIEZE

Sculptured horizontal band in architecture, from the Latin
Phrygium—"from Phrygia," the ancient country in Asia Minor
known for its embroidery.

> The [Temple of Athena Nike] is almost
> square. with four graceful Ionic columns
> at either end. Its frieze, of which only
> fragments remain, consisted of scenes
> from mythology. . .
>
> David Willett, *Greece* (2004)

FUSTIAN

A coarse fabric made of flax and cotton. In the nineteenth century it became exclusively associated with the working classes. It is probably named for El Fostat, a suburb of Cairo, Egypt.

> My hat is but seedy, and fustian's my
>   coat,
> And my trousers are shining with grease,
> My face is unshaven, my hands they
>   denote
> That from labour I scarce ever cease,
>   George Hickling, from "The
>   Man of 'Fustian'" (1861)

G

GALILEE

A porch or chapel at the western entrance of certain medieval churches. Some sources say the name was given because it was located at the less sacred western end and thus likened to the scriptural "Galilee of the Gentiles," Others claim it is because of its location at the far end of the church, as Galilee was the northernmost region of Judea. **Gallery** may be an alteration of galilee.

> Owen and Jehannes walked back towards the guest house in silence, according to the custom of this place, but as they approached the Galilee porch at the west entrance to the church, Jehannes paused. "I would pray," he said,
>> Candace Robb, *The King's Bishop* (1997)

GALOSHES

Waterproof overshoes, from the Latin *gallica (solea)*—"Gaulish (sandal)." Gaul is the name given in antiquity to the region in Europe comprising approximately the territory of modern France and Belgium.

> The Rat left the house and carefully
> examined the muddy surface of the
> ground outside, hoping to find the Mole's
> tracks. There they were, sure enough. The
> galoshes were new, just bought for the
> winter, and the pimples on their soles
> were fresh and sharp. He could see the
> imprints of them in the mud, running
> along straight and purposeful, leading
> direct to the Wild Wood.
>> Kenneth Grahame, *The
>> Wind in the Willows* (1908)

GAMBOGE

Both a film-forming resin and a coloring agent, it was used primarily to tint varnishes but has also been used on its own in watercolors. Bright yellow in color, it comes from a species of trees found in Cambodia and other southeastern Asian countries. It takes its name from *camboja*, an old form of "Cambodia."

> Upon sallying out this morning encount-
> ered the old-fashioned pea soup London
> fog—of a gamboge color. It was lifted,
> however, from the ground & floated in
> mid air. When lower, it was worse.
>> Herman Melville, *Journal of a
>> Tour in London* (1850)

GASCONADE

Boasting, said to be a vice of the Gascons, the inhabitants of Gascony, an area of southwest France.

> There is nothing, however, in the
> Gainsborough picture to suggest
> the awkward manner and occasional
> gasconade which, we are told,
> characterised Wolfe, though much

to indicate the genius and intrepidity
which Pitt discovered in him.
A. E. Fletcher, *Thomas
Gainsborough, B.A.* (1904)

GAUZE

Transparent, loosely-woven fabric. Most likely named after Gaza, where it was supposedly first made.

In Jen the grass is like green silk threads,
in China the mulberry bows beneath its leaves.
Now while your thoughts are turning home,
my longing heart is already breaking.
Oh the spring wind is a stranger to me,
how does it dare to enter my gauze bed curtain
Li Po, "Spring Thoughts" (750)

GERMAN

The german is the original name of the cotillon, a series of party dances popular at nineteenth century balls, and now obsolete. It was said to have originated at the German court of Aix-les-Chapelle, at a ball given to the allied foreigners shortly after the Battle of Waterloo.

The German is the most fashionable dance
in Society. It ends every ball in New York,
Virginia, Boston, Philadelphia, and Newport;
it is a part of the business of life, and
demands consummate skill in its leadership.
Mrs. John Sherwood, *Manners and
Social Usage* (1894)

GEYSER

A natural hot spring that spurts a column of water and steam into the air, the word comes from "Geysir," the name of a hot spring in Iceland, that country's "old Faithful," which, in turn, literally means "gusher" in Icelandic.

> Poetry is the geyser of the unconscious.
> Aleister Crowley,
> *The City of God* (1943)

GHETTO

First used in the sixteenth century to describe a neighborhood in Venice (*campo getto*) on the site of the city's foundry, to which the city's Jews were restricted. Over time it has come to signify a poor, overcrowded, culturally or racially homogenous area. Some etymologists claim that it was not from the Italian name of the foundry, but from "Egypt" (in Latin, *Aegyptus*) because of the Jews' long exile in that land.

> The scope and intensity of ghetto-
> ization in the United States is due
> largely to racial steering and the
> manipulation of housing markets.
> Stanley D. Brunn, *Cities*
> *of the World* (2003)

GILA MONSTER

The poisonous lizard is found in the basin of the Gila River of New Mexico and Arizona.

> What makes this reptile special? The
> Gila monster, and its cousin the Mexican
> beaded lizard, are the only venomous
> carnivorous lizards in the world. If
> startled or cornered, the lizard will attack
> ferociously and hang on with great tenacity.
> Liz Palika, *The Complete Idiot's*
> *Guide to Reptiles & Amphibians*
> (1998)

GOLCONDA

A source of great wealth, especially a mine. From a ruined city of south-central India west of Hyderabad. It was the capital of an ancient kingdom (c. 1364-1512) known for the diamonds found nearby.

> The companies with a stake in the new field on the Utah-Wyoming border hope it will prove to be a several-billion-dollar Golconda.
> *New York Times* (1981)

GRUB STREET

Samuel Johnson in his 1755 *Dictionary* defined it thusly: "a street near Moorfields in London, much inhabited by writers of small histories, dictionaries, and temporary poems, whence any mean production is called grub street." It is sometimes referred to as London's "street of ink."

> Much of Crane's prose was hurried and uneven, produced for Grub Street to survive; yet behind the hack work hovered an idealist who wanted to break out of the narrow newspaper columns and say something larger about human nature
> Herbert Mitgang, *New York Times* (1998)

GUERNSEY

A breed of brown-and-white dairy cattle originally developed on the Isle of Guernsey in the English Channel. Other breeds named for their place of origin include **Aberdeen-Angus**, **Charolais** (Charolle, France), **Devon, Hereford, Holstein, Jersey, Limousin** (region of France), **Maine-Anjou** (river valleys in northwest France), **Simmental** (Simme Valley, Switzerland), **Sussex,** and **Texas Longhorn**.

> There was a farm girl named Maisie
> Who had a cow she named Daisy,
> She gave tasty milk
> And was of that ilk
> Known everywhere as the Guernsey.

GUINEA

Former British gold coin worth one pound and one shilling that was originally made of gold from the Guinea coast of Africa. It is also a derogatory term for an Italian. It was originally *Guinea Negro* and meant black person or person of mixed ancestry. It was applied to Italians in the nineteenth century probably because of their dark complexions relative to northern Europeans. **Guinea pig** is also derived from the African region.

> I would not give half a guinea to live
> under one form of government other
> than another. It is of no moment to
> the happiness of an individual.
> > Samuel Johnson

GYPSY

Alteration of *gypcian,* a Middle English dialect form of *egypcien,* "Egyptian," from the supposed origin of these people. Whether **gyp** (meaning "to cheat') is derived from "Gypsy" (as is commonly thought) is not at all certain.

> There was young girl from Poughkeepsie
> Who ran off with a handsome young gypsy.
> When they got to Albany
> He proposed on bended knee,
> Then they went off and got tipsy.

H

HACKNEY

An English breed of horse first bred in Hackney, a borough of London. It came to also mean a carriage for hire pulled by such a horse. Extended in its abbreviated version—**hack**—to taxicabs and then to a person hired to do routine work.

> I jumped into a hack and went about my business. . . . It was a hack like any other, only a trifle dirtier, with a greasy line along the top of the drab cushions, as if it had been used for a great many Irish funerals.
> Henry James, *The American* (1879)

HAFNIUM

Number 72 on the Periodic Table, it derives its name from *Hafnia*, the Latin name for Copenhagen, Denmark. Other elements named for places include **americium, europium, francium, germanium, polonium, scandium, holmium** (from *Holmia*, the Latinized form of Stock*holm*), **strontium** (from *Strontian*, Scotland), **californium**, and **berkelium**.

> "All I'm aware of is that we are getting illegal shipments of hafnium into the joint company."
> Eric Van Lustbader, *Angel Eyes* (1992)

HALLMARK

A mark of quality, from the official stamps or marks of purity used at London's Goldsmith's *Hall* to denote the purity of silver and gold articles. Over time the word has come to mean, as well, something characteristic of the subject.

> The tight-lipped restraint with which
> long before he had endowed the hero
> of *Mosada* now became a constant
> feature, even a hallmark, of his work.
> Richard Ellmann, *Yeats: The
> Man and the Masks (*1978)

HARRIS TWEED

From the name of the southern section of the island of Lewis with Harris, the largest and northernmost of the Outer Hebrides of Scotland. Originally it referred to fabric produced by the inhabitants there; later it became a proprietary name.

> They found the Harris tweed, this nubby-
> dubby wool cloth, smooth and rough at
> sack, and everywhere these soft little hairs
> riding on top of the weave.
> Carol Shields, *Larry's Party* (1997)

HAVANESE

The only true Cuban breed, it is thought that the small, lively dog's ancestors may have traveled to the island at the time that the Spanish were exploring the Caribbean. The island's capital is also famous for its fine cigars, **Havanas**.

> Fiji was a Havanese, a breed I hadn't known
> existed. It took Jonas a while to settle on a
> name for the puppy. Befitting her heritage,
> Jonas had eventually named his new dog
> after a tropical island. Jonas being Jonas,

he'd chosen an island about as far from the
puppy's ancestral homeland, Cuba, as was
possible
> Stephen White, *The Last Lie*
> (2010)

HAWAIIAN SHIRT

A short-sleeved, loose-fitting shirt originally worn in Hawaii.

Ellery Chun (1909-2000), the owner of King-Smith Clothiers,
a Honolulu store, made from left-over kimono fabric what is
today called the "Hawaiian shirt." He, however, decided to
call it the "aloha" shirt and trademarked the name in 1936.

> The official uniform of gone-to-seed slobs
> worldwide, the Hawaiian shirt (also called
> the "aloha shirt") can conceal a beer gut or
> a salsa stain with equal aplomb—provided
> the pattern is busy enough.
> Sam Stall et al, *The Encyclo-
> pedia of Guilty Pleasures* (2004)

HELOT

A serf or slave, from the name of a class of serfs in ancient
Sparta. The word has been associated with the Laconian town
of Helos whose citizens were enslaved by the Spartans. Today,
it has come to be used to describe individuals in a country who
are illegal entrants, failed asylum seekers, overstayers on visas
and so on, who, as a result, are almost completely lacking
rights, such as the right to due process.

> The status of citizen, denizen or helot are
> increasingly fixed—even generation to
> generation—and the actions of the EU
> are concerned to keep things that way.
> Angus Bancroft, *Roma and
> Gypsy-Travellers in Europe* (2005)

HELVETICA

A sans-serif typeface created by the Swiss in 1957, from the Latin name for Switzerland, *Helvetia*, where it was designed.

> Helvetica is not only the preferred
> typeface of leading professionals, it
> is also an all-time favorite among the
> multitude of codes and signals and
> commands that enliven urban life.
> Helvetica is the perfume of the city.
>> Lars Muller, *Helvetica* (2004)

HENLEY

The collarless pullover shirt is named for Henley-on-Thames in Oxfordshire, England, site of the Royal Regatta, inaugurated in 1839. It was the traditional garb of the rowers.

> He's put on his henley and he's ready to row,
> To race his boat and outdistance his foe.
> He knows that he's gotta
> Go win the regatta
> And won't settle for place or for show.

HESSIAN

The fabric that the English call burlap or sack cloth, takes its name from the state of Hesse in central Germany.

> The writer seemed to have press-ganged
> any material—old sailcloth, edges ripped
> out of God knows what books, burlap,
> even hessian—into use as a surface to
> cover with a colourful, crabbed hand-
> writing that at the best of times was
> hard to decipher
>> Richard Flanagan, *Gould's
>> Book of Fish* (2001)

HISPANIC

An "Hispanic" is defined by the United States Office of Management and Budget as "a person of Mexican, Puerto Rican, Cuban, South or Central American, or other Spanish culture or origin, regardless of race." The term comes from *Hispania*, the Roman name for the Iberian Peninsula.

> Mixed cultural signals have perpetuated
> certain stereotypes—for example, that of
> the Hispanic woman as the "Hot Tamale"
> or sexual firebrand. It is a one-dimensional
> view that the media have found easy to
> promote.
> Judith Ortiz Cofer, *The Latin
> Deli* (1995)

HOCK

A white Rhine wine, short for the German *Hochheimer (wein)*, "(wine of) Hochheim," a village in the Rheingau. Not seen much in the United States since the last century, it still pops up in Britain occasionally.

> We ought to have had Catawba
> wine; but this was wanting, although
> there was plenty of hock, champagne,
> sherry, madeira, port, and claret.
> Nathaniel Hawthorne, *Our
> Old Home* (1863)

HOMBURG

The stiff felt hat was popularized by Edward VII after bringing back one of that style after a visit to Bad Homburg, Germany. It is one of the oldest formal-style hats and was favored by many politicians and diplomats.

> Sedate suits, immaculate chesterfields,
> gray homburgs, thin attaché cases
> grouped in small clusters near the
> doorway of the hotel. The bankers
> were waiting for the cars to take them
> to luncheon or conference, perhaps both.
>> Helen MacInness, *The Salzburg
>> Connection* (1983)

HOOKER

It comes not from General Thomas Hooker, as many believe, but, apparently, according to an 1859 explanation by John Russell Bartlett: "a resident of the Hook, i.e., a strumpet, a sailor's trull, so-called from the number of houses of ill fame frequented by sailors at the Hook (i.e. Corlear's Hook) in the city of New York."

> Miss Barry said one of the biggest
> problems she faces in her work is
> "the happy hooker" image, which
> she believes tends to glorify
> prostitution and make it seem like
> an alternative work experience.
>> Judy Klemesrud, *New York
>> Times* (1985)

I/J

INDIGO

The blue color takes its name from the indigo dye, which, in turn, is named for the plant of that name. The earliest center for the dye was India. Its association is shown in the Greek word for the dye, *indikon,* which eventually came into English as "indigo." The dark black ink known as **india ink** also gets its name from that country, though it actually was invented in China, and in many places is, correctly, called "Chinese ink."

> You ain't been blue, No, No, No,
> You ain't been blue,
> Till you've had that Mood Indigo,
> That feeling' goes stealin' down to
> my shoes,
> While I sit and sigh
> "Go 'long, blues
> From "Mood Indigo,"
> lyric by Irving Mills

IRISH

Its meaning as "temper" or "passion"—as in "get one's Irish up"—comes from the legendary high spirits, if not pugnacity, of the Irish people. "Irish" also shows up in such compound toponyms as "Irish coffee," "Irish setter," and "Irish whiskey."

> "You don't get angry when you
> should. You should be furious at those
> terrible people. I've seen you when you're

angry and aren't you brilliant? But it
takes you a long time to, as you
Yanks say, to get your Irish up."
    "The Irish are a peace-loving
and gentle people" I said. "Well,
most of the time."
        Andrew Greeley, *Irish Whiskey*
        (1998)

ITALIC

The *sloping* typeface's name comes from the Latin *italicus,*
"Italian," and was introduced in 1501 by the Venetian printer
Manutius in an edition of Virgil dedicated to Italy.

    Then Martin, who has a tendency to lean
very hard on words he wants emphasized
—I once wrote that he spoke in italics—
added one last tip of his hat to Stewart:
"He is an *incredible* race car driver."
        Tony Stewart, *True Speed:*
        My Racing Life (2003)

JAPAN

With the small "j," it refers to a black lacquer originating in
Japan, used to produce a glossy finish. **Japonica**, Latin for
Japanese, is a shrub from Japan, grown for its scarlet flowers
and popularly known as a "flowering quince."

    "Japonica glistens like coral in all the
neighboring gardens."
        Henry Reed, "The Naming of
        Things" (1942)

JAVA

Informal name for brewed coffee, from the Indonesian island
of Java, a major coffee exporter.

I love java, sweet and hot.
Whoops! Mr. Moto, I'm a coffee pot.
Shoot me the pot and I'll pour me a shot.
A cup, a cup, a cup, a cup, a cup!
> from "Java Jive" by Ben
> Oakland & Milton Drake

JAVELLE WATER

A solution of sodium or potassium hypochlorite, used as a bleaching agent, and also known as "Javel water" and "eau de Javelle," it takes its name from the former French town of Javel, now part of Paris, where it was first prepared.

> Mildew is rather obstinate, as are iron
> rust and grass stains; Javelle water
> will sometimes obliterate them when
> everything else fails.
> Christine Terhune Herrick,
> *Housekeeping Made Easy*
> (1888)

JEANS

Short for "jean fustian"—that is, fustian fabric from Genoa, Italy. "Blue jeans" are made from blue denim. The Italian port is also the source of a type of sail, the **genoa** (also known as a "jenny"), so named because it was developed by a Swedish yachtsman in 1927 for a race at Genoa.

> If she had to criticize something, she
> might say that his jeans were a tad too
> tight. Then again, if one was going to
> seduce European men, tight jeans were
> an occupational hazard.
> Lauren Weisberger, *Chasing
> Harry Winston* (2008)

JERSEY

There are at least three meanings of the word: (1) a pullover sweater or shirt, such as worn by athletic teams; (2) a fine knitted fabric, slightly stretchy; and (3) a breed of dairy cattle. All get their name from the island of Jersey, one of England's Channel Islands. The pullover was originally a woolen sweater peculiar to the fishermen of the island.

> The difference between the old ballplayer
> and the new ballplayer is the jersey. The
> old ballplayer cared about the name on the
> front. The new ballplayer cares about the
> name on the back.
>> Steve Garvey, former L.A. Dodger

JET

A deep-black-colored coal or color, from French *geet,* by way of the Greek *gagates lithos* or "stone of Gages," a town in the ancient land of Lycia on the southwestern coast of Asia Minor.

> Jet-black cats with golden eyes
> Shadows black as ink,
> Firelight blinking in the dark
> With a yellow blink.
>> Nancy Byrd Turner
>> from "Black and Gold"

JEW

The name originally meant a "Hebrew of the Kingdom of Judea," the ancient land of southern Palestine occupied by the tribes of Judah, the son of Jacob and Leah.

> The phrase "funny but you don't look Jewish"
> has become a punch line without need of a story.
> An example tells of an orthodox Jewish
> businessman who was in China on Yom Kippur
> and desired to attend services. He inquired about

and learned of a Orthodox synagogue. It took him
hours to locate it but one there he was amazed to
find Chinese worshippers and a Chinese rabbi.
After the service he went over to the rabbi and
exclaimed that it was one of the finest he had ever
attended. The rabbi looked him over and asked,
"Ah so, are you Jewish?" "Of course I'm Jewish.,"
the man said in a pained way. "Funny," said the
rabbi, "you don't look Jewish."

Sarah Blacher Cohen, *Jewish Wry*:
Essays on Jewish Humor (1990)

JODHPURS

Long riding breeches, tight from the knee to ankle, named
after the ancient city of Jodhpur in the state of Rajasthan in
North India where the local men wear such trousers.

And this perfume of saddlery itself, and
this powder of a sorrel horse that
every night, in dreams,
The hand of the Horseman passes across
his face again, can it arouse
within us no other dream
Than your tawny image of riders, O
tender companions of our rides, whose
jodhpurs are imbued with the
perfume of your bodies?
Saint-John Perse, from
"Vents/Winds"

JURASSIC

Designating the time and limestone deposits of the second
period of the Mesozoic era, characterized by the presence of
dinosaurs. The name comes from the Jura, a range of
mountains along the French-Swiss border, where such mineral
deposits were discovered.

The rocks here in the part of Dorset . . .
were all . . . laid down during the period
known as the Jurassic.

> Simon Winchester, *The Map
> That Changed the World* (2002)

K/L

KARAKUL

A very old breed of domesticated sheep and named after a village situated in the valley of the Amu Darja River in the province of Bukhara in Uzbekistan. A hat made from its fur is popular with Muslim men in Central Asia.

> The men who wear suits or modern dress opt
> for a wool hat called a *karakul* that is made of
> lamb's wool and has the shape of a flat khaki
> army cap. Looks quite distinguished.
> Eloise Hanner, *Letters from*
> *Afghanistan* (2003)

KERSEY

A heavy fabric used for uniforms, coats, and stockings, it originated in Kersey, Sussex, in the 11th century where its manufacture was the mainstay of western England cloth production for centuries.

> Henceforth my wooing mind shall be express'd
> in russet yeas and honest kersey noes.
> William Shakespeare, *Love's Labours*
> *Lost* (1598)

KREMLIN

The personification of the Russian government. The actual Kremlin is a fortified complex in Moscow that houses the offices of the government. The name comes from a Tatar word for "citadel."

> To those, who have seen the hand of
> the Kremlin behind all this master
> strategy, it must be clear by now that if
> the objective of the Communists in
> Southeast Asia was to see the United
> States sacrifice men and money in tre-
> mendous quantities while they them-
> selves gave up little money and no men,
> Vietnam was the ideal situation.
>> L. Fletcher Prouty, *JFK: The*
>> *CIA, Vietnam and the Plot to*
>> *Assassinate John F. Kennedy*
>> (1996)

KRIMMER

A type of fur taken from young lambs of the Crimean region.

Krimmer is German for *Crimean*.

> More common that ermine, but
> almost as as pretty is the long-
> haired Angora lamb, while beaver
> and krimmer, which are much
> worn by older children, are among
> the most serviceable and least
> costly of fur garnitures.
>> *Godey's Magazine* (1894)

LABRADOR

The Labrador retriever, or "Lab," actually developed in Newfoundland, from whence it made his way to England, probably with fishermen who worked the Canadian fisheries. There, in order to avoid confusion with the larger, heavy-coated Newfoundland dog, it was called the Labrador after the peninsula which contains mainland Newfoundland.

Bill wanted a big dog he could run with. We worked through that and finally decided that a Labrador would be just the right size and temperament for our family and the White House.

I wanted to give the dog to Bill as a Christmas present, so I set out to locate the perfect puppy. In early December, a bouncing three-month-old chocolate Lab met the President for the first time. The puppy scampered straight into Bill's arms, and they fell in love on the spot.

Hillary Rodham Clinton, *Living History* (2003)

LACONIC

Terse or concise in language. It literally means "of or relating to the Spartans," the natives of Laconia, the ancient region of the Greek Peloponnesus, known for their brevity of speech.

You can get far in North America with laconic grunts. "Huh," "hun," and "hi!" in their various modulations, together with "sure," "guess so," "that so?" and "nuts!" will meet almost any contingency.

Ian Fleming

LANDAU

A four-wheeled carriage with facing front-and-back passenger seats and a roof made in two sections for lowering or detachment. It was made in Landau, Bavaria, Germany.

As I am coming back through Tottenham Road, I see a landau before me, and on the box-seat by the driver is my young friend Charley, who waves his hat to me. I ran up to the carriage, my knees knocking together so that I thought I should fall by the wheel . . .

William M. Thackerey, *The Virginians* (1857)

LANGLEY

The personification of the Central Intelligence Agency which has its offices at Langley, Virginia.

> "We've got new orders from Langley. Guevara goes down. They don't care how it gets done We do whatever it takes to get Bolivians into the field."
> "Is this Langley talking, or are you just bucking for a corner office?"
> "Both," Smith said. "Langley wants this thing pinched off before it becomes a full blown civil war. If the Bolivians won't stomp the Cubans, we will."
> Chuck Pfarrer, *Killing Che* (2008)

LATEEN

A rig used on the north coast of Africa and characterized by a triangular sail extended by a long spar slung to a low mast, from the Italian and Spanish *vela Latina*—"Latin sail—as it was commonly used in the Mediterranean. See "Latin," below.

> The wind upon our quarter lies,
> And on before the freshening gale,
> That fills the snow-white lateen sail,
> Swiftly our light felucca flies.
> Henry Wadsworth Longfellow, from "The Golden Legend" (1851)

LATIN

A person from Latin America. "Latin" comes from "Latium," the ancient country in west-central Italy that was home to the original Latin people, who believed that they were descendants of Latinus, the father-in-law of Aeneas. In the United States "Latino" seems to have replaced "Latin."

> She's a Latin from Manhattan
> I can tell by her 'Man-ya-na"
> She's a Latin from Manhattan
> But not Havana
> Though she does the rhumba for us
> And she calls herself Dolores
> She was in a Broadway chorus
> Known as Suzy Donahue
> She can take her tambourine and
>   whack it
> But to her it's just a racket
> She's a hoofer from Tenth Avenue
>   From "She's a Latin from
>   Manhattan" (words by Al
>   Dubin)

LAVALIERE

A pendant worn on a chain around the neck. It was named after Mademoiselle de la Lavalliere (1644-1710), *née* Louise de la Baume le Blanc, a mistress of Louis XIV. Chateau-la-Valliere, in central France, was made a duchy in her favor upon the legitimization of her children by the king in 1667. Once popular among college students, today it is more likely seen in the context of cordless microphones.

> I remember in college when my
> fraternity brother told me he wanted
> to "lavaliere" his girl friend.
> Having never heard of the term I
> thought he meant to practice some
> kind of French perversion.
>   William Betcher,
>   *Intimate Play* (1987)

LEGHORN

The name of both a kind of plaited straw hat and a chicken, it comes from Leghorn, an anglicism for the Tuscan port of Livorno, previously named Legorno. The hat, made of woven wheat fiber, was exported from Leghorn. It is also where the toponymous chicken was first bred and went on to be the leading egg producer of the world.

> I seem to remember that, with that [blue]
> dress, she wore an immensely broad
> leghorn hat—like the Chapeau de Paille
> of Rubens, only very white. The hat would
> be tied with lightly knotted scarf of the
> same stuff as her dress. She knew how to
> give value to her blue eyes.
> Ford Madox Ford, *The Good*
> *Soldier* (1915)

LESBIAN

Relating to sexual relations between women, from the Greek *Lesbius*, "of Lesbos," the island in the Aegean Sea, once home to the lyric poet Sappho. Whether she was in fact homosexual has never been established; but, as etymologist Eric Partridge has written, "slander has foisted upon her this practice, maybe on account of the amorous ardor of some of her poems."

> Lesbianism was once a risque word.
> Euphemisms were used instead.
> "Sapphic liaison" is one that was
> heard
> And understood by those who read.
> But no need for such evasions today;
> It's a time when one simply can say
> "gay."

LHASA APSO

It is the most popular dog breed indigenous to Tibet. *Apso* means "goat-like" and "long hair" in Tibetan and *Lhasa* refers to the capital city of Tibet, where they were used as watch dogs in the temples and monasteries.

> On her weekend visits, Lily was permitted to bring the family dog, Flour, along. One day, during a thunderstorm, someone saw Vonnegut taking the little Lhasa apso for a walk. He followed behind, holding out an umbrella at arm's length to keep her dry as she skipped about his feet, while the rain poured down on him instead.
>
> Charles J. Shields, *And So It Goes*: Kurt Vonnegut: A Life (2011)

LIMERICK

The five-line nonsense verse might have originated in the city and county of Limerick, Ireland, but the nexus is obscure. Some are of the opinion that the name came from a now-lost refrain that was sung between limericks, that included the line "Will you come up to Limerick?

> The limerick is furtive and mean;
> You must keep her in close quarantine,
> Or she sneaks to the slums
> And properly becomes
> Disorderly, drunk and obscene.
> Morris Bishop

LIMOGES

A variety of fine porcelain made at Limoges, France, sometimes known as "Limoges ware."

> From the hand-painted jam jars to the
> Limoges teacups, and from the custom-

blended teas to the Frette linens, the
Peninsula Hotel's afternoon tea is
without question the Beverly Hills
rendition of the traditional English
high tea.
> Merle Elias, *Los Angeles*
> *First Class* (2001)

LIMOUSINE

A large passenger automobile, usually driven by a chauffeur. The original limousine (1902) had an enclosed passenger compartment and an open but roofed driver's seat. The driver's section was said to resemble the hood of a kind of flowing mantle or coat, popularized in Limousin, a region and former province of west-central France.

> He was tall, about fifty, with darkly
> handsome, almost sinister features: a
> neatly trimmed mustache, hair turning
> silver at the temples, and eyes so black
> they were like the tinted windows of a
> sleek limousine—he could see out, but
> you couldn't see in.
> > John Berendt, *Midnight in the*
> > *Garden of Good and Evil*
> > (1994)

LINSEY-WOOLSEY

A coarse fabric first made in Lindsey, England, of wool combined with flax or cotton.

> The truly fashionable gentleman of
> those days—his dress, which served
> for both morning and evening, street
> and drawing-room, was a linsey-woolsey
> coat, made, perhaps, by the fair hands of
> the mistress of his affections.
> > Washington Irving,

LISLE

A smooth fine cotton thread used for making stockings, gloves, and underwear. It is named after the town of Lisle— now Lille—in northern France where it was originally made in the sixteenth century.

> As everyone knows
> Lisle is used in hose—
> And some other clothes
> I suppose.

LOVAGE

A European herb used as a food seasoning. The name comes from *levisticum* (*apium*) "Ligurian (parsley)." Liguria is a region of Italy along the northwestern coast.

> Lovage, which is similar to a wild celery,
> is a wonderful addition to any herb garden,
> and it literally grows like a weed. . . . It is
> especially good in soups in which its celery
> taste plays an important role. Both the
> deep green stalks and the leaves of lovage
> add immeasurably to the flavor and
> appearance of any dish.
> > Lois Anne Rothert, *The Soups of
> > France* (2002)

LUMBER

In England "lumber" refers to useless furniture, often stored in a "lumber-room." Probably derived from "Lombard Street," where the Italian immigrants from Lombardy had their moneylending and banking houses in the thirteenth century and stored the myriad objects which had been pawned. In America "lumber" is used for roughly sawed timber.

> Often and often Nicholas had pictured to
> himself what the lumber-room might be
> like, that region that was so carefully
> sealed from youthful eyes and concerning
> which no questions were ever answered.
> Saki, "The Lumber-Room"
> (1914)

LUNATIC

It means to be insane (or one who is insane), literally to be "moon-struck." From *Luna*, the Latin word for the moon. Of course, one can be effected by the moon without being a lunatic, can be merely **moony,** or dreamy.

> The lunatic may be "soothed," . . . for
> a time, but in the end he is very apt to
> become obstreperous. His cunning, too,
> is proverbial and great. When a madman
> appears thoroughly sane, indeed, it is
> high time to put him in a straight jacket.
> Edgar Allan Poe, "The
> System of Doctor Tarr and
> Professor Fether" (1845)

LYME DISEASE

The bacterial illness spread by ticks debuted in 1975 when the parents of a group of children who lived near each other in Lyme, Connecticut, made researchers aware that their children had all been diagnosed with rheumatoid arthritis. This unusual grouping eventually led researchers to the identification of the bacterial cause of the children's condition, what was then called "Lyme disease" in 1982.

Some people believe Lyme disease is a

new disease. That is not really true. The
bacteria that cause Lyme disease have
been making people sick for a long time.
But Lyme disease was not identified and
named until 1975. Before that, the sympt-
oms were confused with other illnesses.
People who had Lyme disease did not get
the right kind of treatment and often kept
getting sicker

> Karen Donnelly, *Everything You
> Need to Know About Lyme
> Disease* (2000)

LYONNAISE

In cuisine, it means "cooked with onions" as in the famous
dish of Lyonnaise potatoes. Its literal meaning is "in the
manner of Lyon," the French city renowned for its gastronomy
and its elevation of the lowly onion to lofty heights

> Mother knew the potatoes she fried with
> onions were called Lyonnaise potatoes,
> after a place in France, from having
> gone to dinner with the Jacobs, but I
> had just learned it. I thought from
> then on we should always call them
> that.
> "You should say, 'We are
> having Lyonnaise potatoes for
> supper, children.'"

> Fannie B. Erickson, *The Blue
> Roof: A Memoir of the 1930s
> in Little Rock* (2007)

M

MACKINAW

Short double-breasted coat of heavy woolen material, usually plaid. from "Mackinac," the island in Michigan on Lake Huron. The coat was a trading item through the entrepot on the island in the nineteenth century.

> The first winter he wore moccasins
> that were born yellow, but after many
> applications of oil and dirt assumed
> their mature color, a dirty, greenish
> brown; he wore a gray plaid mackinaw
> coat, and a red toboggan cap.
> F. Scott Fitzgerald, *This Side*
> *of Paradise* (1920)

MADEIRA

The fortified wine is named after the mid-Atlantic Portuguese island where it is made.

> Have some Madeira, m'dear!
> It's very much nicer than Beer;
> I don't care for Sherry, one cannot
> drink Stout,
> and Port is a wine I can well do without;
> It's simply a case of Chacun à son GOUT!
> Have some Madeira, m'dear!'
> From "Madeira, M'Dear"
> by Flanders & Swann (1957)

MADISON AVENUE

The methods of advertising, from the street in Manhattan known as the center of the American advertising business.

> Madison Avenue should be commended,
> and then flogged, on the brainwashing of
> America, as we all seem to have jumped
> on board the "buying things says 'I love
> you'" train.
>> Paul B. Schmidt, *Burlington*
>> *Free Press* (2007)

MADRAS

A cotton cloth, often striped or plaid or checked patterned. It was originally produced in Madras, India.

> There was an Old Man of Madras,
> Who rode on a cream-coloured ass;
> But the length of its ears,
> So promoted his fears,
> That it killed that Old Man of Madras.
>> Edward Lear, *Book of*
>> *Nonsense* (1846)

MADRILENE

Literally meaning "of Madrid" in French, it refers to a tomato-flavored consommé, usually served chilled in a jellied form.

> "They are in town from the
> suburbs, and in a minute they will
> all order consommé madrilène.
> People from suburbs always order
> consommé madrilène as soon as
> they see it on the menu."
> Immediately, from amid
> the murmur of voices, I can hear
> the words, "Consommé madrilène,"
> spoken with a little complacency.
> I am filled with astonishment
> and admiration.

Thomas Merton, *My
Argument With the
Gestapo* (1975)

MAFFICK

To rejoice with boisterous public demonstrations. It is a back-formation from Mafeking, referring to the wild celebration of the raising of the siege of Mafeking, South Africa in 1900. Though seldom used in the United States, it shows up occasionally in England and the Commonwealth countries..

> "It's a fact of life, though, isn't it?"
> he went on. "Whenever people are
> let loose before they're ready, they
> maffick about like a pack of hyenas
> smelling blood."
> Keith Heller, *The Woman
> Who Knew Gandhi* (2004)

MAGENTA

From the town in northern Italy where an internecine battle was fought in 1859 during the Second War of Italian Independence. Afterward, "magenta" was adopted to describe a purplish red, characteristic of the bloodiness of the battle.

> Here in the canyon you'd think there
> was blazing fire everywhere. The vines
> and the maples are red, scarlet, carmine,
> cerise, magenta, all the hues of flame.
> Zane Grey, *The Call of the
> Canyon* (1924)

MAGNET

The ancients found a certain hard, black stone at Magnesia in northern Greece, which they called "magnet," and discovered that it attracted small pieces of iron. They thought that it possessed some magic property and it became very famous. It was not discovered until about the eleventh century that the stone would take a north and south position when it was hung up by a string. The names of the elements **magnesium** and **manganese**, as well as the compound **milk of magnesia**, come from the same source.

> He added that she head a magnetic personality,
> that she radiated health and joy. He thought it
> might be well to cultivate her acquaintance,
> she made him feel good.
> Henry Miller, *Big Sur and the*
> *Oranges of Hieronymus Bosch* (1957)

MAJOLICA

A kind of richly colored and decorated Italian Renaissance pottery that is enameled and glazed. The word is a medieval form of "Majorca," the Spanish Balearic island, where the ceramic style supposedly originated.

> Dressed in a thin white chemise with a
> geometrically patterned blue shawl falling
> about her waist, Isabella stands leaning
> over a large painted majolica pot that
> sprouts a thick clump of basil and rests on
> a richly embroidered cloth adorning a
> prie-dieu inlaid with ivory and precious
> stones.
> James A. W. Heffernan,
> *Cultivating Picturacy* (2006)

MALINES

A fine lace in which the pattern details are defined by a flat thread, from Malines, the French name for Mechlin, Belgium, where the lace was originally woven. It is also called **mechlin**.

> In "Roderick Random" the fops,
> naval and military, of the day have
> their hair powdered with maréchal,
> and wear cambric shirts with Malines
> lace dyed with coffee-grounds.
>> Mrs. Bury Palliser, *History
>> of Lace* (1865)

MALL

Before it became identified with "shopping mall," it referred to a public walk—such as The Mall in London. It, in turn, was named after an Italian croquet-like game, *pallamaglio*, which the English called "pall-mall." A field was built on St. James's Park and named after the game. The shopping complexes we call malls were not so named until the 1960s.

> The teens of the 1980s inspired a
> slew of shopping words. The
> unprecedented amount of time
> this generation of Valley Girls and
> their guys spent at the mall resulted
> in terms *mall rat*, *mallie*, and
> *shopaholic* in the early '80s.
>> Pamela Klaffke, *Spree:
>> A Cultural History of
>> Shopping* (2003)

MALMSEY

A sweet fortified white wine originally made in Greece, from *Monembasia*, the Greek seaport from which it was shipped.

> Several yeoman came forward and
> spread cloths upon the green grass,
> and placed a royal feast; while others
> still broached barrels of sack and
> Malmsey and good stout ale, and set
> them in jars upon the cloth, with
> drinking-horns about them. Then all

sat down and feasted and drank
merrily together until the sun was
low and the half-moon glimmered
with a pale light betwixt the leaves
of the trees overhead.

> Howard Pyle, *The Merry*
> *Adventures of Robin Hood*
> (1883)

MALTESE

This little dog was described by an early writer as belonging to the "Melita" breed, an archaic name for Malta. It was developed in Italy with the addition of miniature spaniel and poodle blood. It is believed that they were brought to England by Crusaders returning home from the Mediterranean.

> In the middle of the floor, to the left of the
> Saint's desk, a little Maltese dog sits bolt
> upright. He is bathed with celestial light, to
> which he pays no attention as he stares at his
> master in an attitude of absolute expectation.
>
> Harry Matthews, *The Case of the*
> *Persevering Maltese* (2003)

MANHATTAN

The genesis of the famous cocktail named after the New York City borough is not clear. The popular myth that it was spawned at a banquet at the Manhattan Club in the 1870s has been pretty much debunked.

> He and Charley stood a long time
> drinking Manhattans at a dark-paneled
> bar in a group of white-haired old
> gents with a barroom tan on their faces.
>
> John Dos Passos, *The Big*
> *Money* (1936)

MANILA

The name for the yellowish hue comes from the color of Manila paper—used in the familiar Manila folder—originally made of hemp from the Philippines capital of Manila.

> Other, larger photos hung behind, nearly
> obscuring the flowered wallpaper that
> had darkened over the years to the color
> of a manila envelope.
>> Anne Tyler, *Saint Maybe* (1992)

MANX

The tailless cat is believed to have originated hundreds of years ago on the English Isle of Man, a native of which is called a "Manx."

> The Manx cat comes from the
>> Isle of Man,
> Where the winter is colder and
>> drearier.
> And while all Manx cats have a
>> nice fur coat,
> Some are dreadfully short-changed
>> in the derriere.
>> Calvin N. Smith, From
>> "Let Us Give Thanx for
>> the Manx" (2004)

MARATHON

"Marathon race" is derived from the story of the fifth century B.C. Greek hero who ran the twenty-six miles and 385 yards to Athens from the Plains of Marathon to give news of the victory of the Greeks over the Persian army. Today a marathon can mean any long event.

> Bellow's other device for creating an
> illusion of space is the introduction of

the grotesque as spellbinding, marathon
talker. All his life Bellow has been
fascinated by authoritative orators of all
varieties—by eloquent cranks, hucksters,
confidence men, and city-park haranguers.
Earl Rovit, Saul Bellow (1967)

MARSALA

Marsala wine originated in the city of Marsala in Sicily. The
English trader John Woodhouse, after tasting the local wine,
soon realized its economic potential. He set up a business in
the 1770's in Marsala to export it to England.

> He comes once more to twit us about
> wine. So much so that the Cagliari
> girl orders a glass of Marsala: and I
> must second her. So there we are,
> three little glasses of brown liquid.
> D. H. Lawrence, Sea and
Sardinia (1921)

MARTINGALE

There are a couple of meanings. The most common is a part
of a harness made to prevent a horse from throwing back its
head. It can also refer to a loose half-belt or strap placed on
the back of coat or jacket. It is from the French *chausses a la
martingale*—trousers in the manner of a native of Martigue, a
small village in Provence (whose natives fasten their trousers
at the back).

> Our coachman had him harnessed
> in as tight and strong as he could,
> with the martingale, and the bearing
> rein, a very sharp curb, and the reins
> put in at the bottom bar. It is my
> belief that that it made the horse mad.
> Anna Sewell. Black Beauty (1904)

114

MASSASAUGA

The North American venomous snake was first discovered

along the Massasauga River in Ontario, Canada.

> A cold coiled liner of mottled lead,
> He lies where grazing cattle tread,
> And lifts a fanged and spiteful head.
>
> His touch is deadly, and his eyes
> Are hot with hatred and surprise—
> Death waits and watches where he lies!
> From "The Massasauga" by
> Hamlin Garland (1899)

MAUDLIN

Excessively sentimental, from (Mary) Magdalene, who is
usually depicted as tearful. "Magdalene" means "of
Magdalen," Mary's home place near Tiberias on the western
shore of Galilee.

> The veteran Japanese choreographer
> Mika Kurosawa must inspire eye-rolling
> envy among other performers. She
> captivates when she does very little. She
> captivates when she does nothing. She
> captivates when she scurries offstage,
> leaving her audience staring at the detritus
> of a solo while one of the most syrupy
> pop songs ever written runs its maudlin
> course.
> Claudia La Rocco, *New York
> Times* (2007)

MAZURKA

The name of a polka-like dance which originally meant a
person from Mazovia province of Poland, where it originated.

Four couples were already executing a
dashing mazurka; their heels pounded
the floor, while the army staff captain
had thrown himself body and soul—not
to mention arms and legs—into the
dance and was cutting capers more
outlandish than any you could see in
your wildest dreams.
> Nikolai Gogol, *Dead Souls*
> (1842)

MEANDER

A verb meaning to "follow a turning and winding course." It
comes from Maiandros, a river in the ancient country of
Phrygia in west-central Asia Minor (settled in 13th century
B.C.), noted for its tortuous course.

> Her sentences meander from *étrangeté*
> to *bizarrerie*, dislocating metaphor
> and being 'easily carried away' in this
> language which is dictated by no
> consciousness, and leaving a reader
> stranded in flight from multivalent
> realities.
> Thomas Docherty, *Alterities*
> (1996)

MECCA

A place of pilgrimage, after the holy city in Saudi Arabia,
destination of Moslem pilgrims.

> I remember one holiday when the
> Williams clan . . . stumbled over each
> other getting into the assortment of cars
> lining the semicircular driveway of the
> big family house and headed for South
> DeKalb Mall, black Atlanta's shopping
> mecca, for our day-after Christmas
> shopping spree.

Colleen Sell, *A Cup of Comfort* (2003)

MEISSEN WARE

A delicate porcelain ware made in Meissen, Germany. In England it is often called "Dresden china," after the city some twenty kilometers from Meissen.

> Miss Tenant is small and fragile
> as bewitching and brittle as a
> Meissen figurine.
>> John Hersey, *The Call*
>> (1985)

MICHIGAN ROLL

A large and ostentatious bankroll consisting of many low-denomination notes wrapped around with one large note. In *A Vocabulary of Criminal Slang*, published in 1914, the noun "Michigan" is said to be slang for "spectacular ruse; a deceptive appearance, as a fake bank roll; a hoax started with sinister intent." Why Michigan? Who knows? Eric Partridge in his *A Dictionary of the Uunderworld* (1950) states that it is "merely one of those State-rivalry amenities."

> "Lady, If I wanted to screw you . . .
> you'd have found a Michigan sandwich
> in that bag the other day." A Michigan
> sandwich, also known as a Michigan roll
> or brick, was a thick sheaf of bills with
> twenties or hundreds on the outside,
> depending on the size of the con, and
> singles or green paper cut to the size of
> currency on the inside.
>> Jonathan Nasaw, *When She Was Bad* (2007)

MILLINER

A person who makes women's hats. It is an alteration of *Milaner*, a native of Milan, Italy, known as an importer of goods, such as women's finery.

> He was perfumed like a milliner,
> And 'twixt his finger and his thumb
> he held
> A pounced-box, which ever and anon
> He gave his nose, and took 't away again.
> William Shakespeare, *Henry IV*
> *Part 1* (1598)

MOCHA

It originally referred to coffee beans shipped from the port of Mocha ("Al-Mukha"), on the Arabian Peninsula in what is now called Yemen. There, just across the Red Sea from Ethiopia, where coffee trees grew wild, coffee was first cultivated and commercialized. Today "mocha" is used to describe anything with the combination of coffee and chocolate.. It can also mean a shade of dark brown.

> Marta Burrell was from Barbados, a
> mocha-skinned woman of thirty-
> eight, tall and slender as a fashion
> model with an air of sultry
> indifference. . . .
> Joseph Finder, *Company*
> *Man* (2005)

MONADNOCK

A rocky mass or mountain that has resisted erosion and stands isolated. It is named after such a mountain, Mount Monadnock, in New Hampshire.

> The boulder-strewn cliff that Hemingway

referred to on page 7 in The Short Happy
Life of Francis Macomber could be
similar to a monadnock. A monadnock is a hill, mountain, or mound
of resistant rock surmounting a
peneplain. Monadnocks are common
features in Africa.

> Henry Mount, *Hemingway's*
> *Tribute to Soil* (2006)

MONEY

The genesis of the modern English words "money" and "mint"
lie in ancient Rome, where coins were struck near the temple
of the goddess Juno Moneta, located on the Capitol. The
goddess's name, Moneta (*Warner* or *Reminder* in Latin)
ultimately came to mean the place where the coins were made,
that is, the "mint," and to its product, "money."

> Money, money, money
> Must be funny
> In the rich man's world
> Money, money, money
> Always sunny
> In he rich man's world
> Aha-ahaaa
> All the things I could do
> If I had a little money
> It's a rich man's world
> > From "Money, Money,
> > Money" (1976) (Anders-
> > son & Uylvaeus) record-
> > ed by ABBA

MONGOLOID

A major ethnic division of the human race, whose members
are characterized by yellowish-brown to white pigmentation
and coarse straight black hair. From "Mongolia," a region of

east-central Asia. **Mongolism** is a congenital disability in which a child is born with a short, flattened skull, slanting eyes, and other anomalies; from a supposed resemblance to the features of ethnic Mongoloids.

> British scientists working in Mexico discovered two skulls, both older than 12,000 years, which appeared to be Caucasoid. Dr. Silvia Gonzales . . . says, "It looks like some of the most ancient native Americans were not of Mongoloid affinity and therefore perhaps not directly related to modern Native Americans."
>> Kathleen O'Neal Gear & W. Michael Gear, *People of the Raven* (2004)

MOROCCO

A soft leather of goatskin, made originally in Morocco, used chiefly for shoes and bookbindings.

> James I was the first of our sovereigns whose books were, as a rule, bound in morocco leather. Morocco is made from the skin of the goat, and for beauty and durability it far excels all other leathers.
>> *The Anglo-Saxon Review* (1899)

MUSCOVY

This waterfowl is often called Muscovy Duck, a folk etymology from "musk duck" by mistaken association with Muscovy, the ancient name of Moscow, Russia. **Muscovite,** a mineral, often called "isinglass," is the common mica which in the form of clear or slightly smoky-colored sheets is used for the opening of stoves and lanterns and even for the windows of houses in some regions where glass is difficult to come by; It was the last use in Russia that gave the name to the mineral of "Muscovy glass," hence the mineralogical name of Muscovite

> The Muscovy duck, more properly called
> musk duck, . . is supposed to have origin-
> ally come from South America, whence it
> has spread over the world.
>> George Ripley, *The New American*
>> *Cyclopaedia* (1859)

MUSLIN

Any of various cotton fabrics, used especially for sheets, from Italian *mussolina*, "cloth of Mosul,' as it was originally made in Al-Mawsil, known today as Mosul, Iraq.

> "She makes me feel what a child must
> feel who goes to a party wearing blacked
> leather buttoned boots and a serge dress,
> when all the other children are dressed in
> muslin and lace and white satin shoes."
>> Mary C. E. Wemyss, *Impossible*
>> *People* (1918)

N/O

NANKEEN

A durable yellowish cotton cloth. originally imported from
the former capital city of Nanjing, China.

> A practical cloth is nankeen.
> It's sturdy and easy to clean.
> The texture is rough,
> The color is buff,
> Yet it has a rather nice sheen.

NAPOLEON

The wonderful mille-feuille pastry has nothing to do with
Bonaparte; rather it is the French word for Neapolitan—
napolitain—"of Naples," Italy, where the tasty treat
presumably was first concocted.

> There are favorite ways to eat Napoleons.
> If you can open your mouth widely enough,
> bite down from the top. Be careful! You
> might get a noseful of whipped cream, but
> who cares. The taste is very satisfying.
> Alice Borning, *Reminiscences of*
> *a Baker's Daughter* (2010)

NASSAU

A popular golf bet, essentially three bets in one: the front nine,
the back nine, and eighteen-hole scores count as separate bets.
It was invented in 1900 at the Nassau Country Club in Nassau

County, in Long Island, New York. It has nothing to do with the Bahamas.

> The Lyons-Krock team were pressing for
> a Nassau bet of five dollars—that is to say
> five dollars bet on the outcome of the first
> nine, five dollars on the second, and five
> dollars on the winner of the match—press
> bets, of course, which meant that the team
> behind could accept a loss and renew the
> wager for the remaining holes.
> George Plimpton, *The Bogey
> Man* (1968)

NATRON

In ancient times this complex admixture of sodium carbonate and sodium bicarbonate was scraped from the Egyptian salt lake deposits in the wadi Natrum, which provided the substance with its modern name. It was an ingredient of soap and acted as the embalming agent for mummification. Because the original name of the element sodium was *natrium* (chemical symbol "Na") there are many names of mineral varieties with *natron* as a part of the name. This means only that they contain sodium.

> Mummification basically involves the
> desiccation of the body using common salt
> or natron that draws out the bodily fluids
> leaving the dry husk.
> Salima Ikram, *Divine Creatures*
> (2005)

NAUGAHYDE

A nylon-coated fabric having the appearance, feel, and flexibility of leather. It gets its name not because cute little naugas were slaughtered to make it, but because it was developed by Uniroyal Engineered Products, Inc. at Naugatuck, Connecticut. Although a proprietary name, sometimes it can be spotted in a lower-case generic form for simulated leather.

> I had a black Naugahyde couch I
> always put in the living room, despite
> the fact some liberal got up a drive to
> do away with Naugahyde couches
> because of the number of little Naugas
> they had to hit in the head with lead
> pipes to make even one Naugahyde
> ottoman.
>> Lewis Grizzard, *Getting It On*
>> (1989)

NEANDERTHAL

A slang term for a crude person. It alludes to "Neanderthal man," an extinct species that lived during the late Pleistocene age. It was identified in 1856 from remains found in the *Neanderthal*, near Dusseldorf, Germany. It literally means "Neander Valley" in German.

> Andrea glared at me through her bangs.
> I returned her look with a hearty "What?"
> and a shrug of the shoulders. "I don't
> like your boyfriend. You're dating a
> Neanderthal."
>> Joe Peacock, *Mentally
>> Incontinent* (2005)

NELSON

This wrestling pressure hold—and its brother, the half-nelson—is believed to take its name from a town by that name in Lancashire, England, once popular for its wrestling matches. Others, however, claim that it is named after a wrestler who devised the hold.

> I felt like getting old Stradlater in
> a half nelson. That's a wrestling
> hold, in case you don't know,
> where you get the other guy
> around the neck and choke
> him to death, if you feel like it.
> > J. D. Salinger, *The Catcher*
> > *in the Rye* (1951)

NEWFOUNDLAND

The breed is thought to have originated in Newfoundland, Canada, from dogs indigenous to the island and the big black bear dogs introduced by the Vikings in 1001 A.D.

> Some presidential dogs were given
> official positions or performed useful
> services during their master's term
> of office. Faithful, the powerful
> Newfoundland pup of Ulysses Grant's
> son, was appointed a White House
> steward in order to intimidate the
> servants, who the President suspected
> of poisoning his children's pets.
> > Roy Rowan, *First Dogs* (2009)

NIAGARA

A flood or torrent, an allusion to "Niagara Falls," the great waterfall on the United States/Canadian border.

> Other Daoists, as well, equally convinced
> of the impossibility of capturing the eternal,
> shape-shifting Truth in evanescent shackles
> of words, kept writing with the result that
> we have a torrent, a niagara, of recorded
> words in the Daoist canon . . . .
> > Robert Ford Campany, *To Live*
> > *as Long as Heaven and Earth*
> > (2002)

NILE GREEN

This yellowish shade of green is supposedly the same hue as the surface water of Africa's longest river, the Nile. In the fashion world it is often called *eau de Nil*.

> The river took on a greenish hue, which
> I was told is actually called "Nile green"
> because there is no other shade in the
> world exactly like it.
>> Margaret George, *The Memoirs*
>> *Of Cleopatra: A Novel* (1998)

NORWAY RAT

The common brown rat did not originate in Norway. It seems to have been named erroneously by the English who thought they were imported by Norwegian ships. In fact, they came from Asia and did not arrive in Europe until the 16th century.

> The public believed that the brown
> rat came from Norway, and to this
> day, among the vulgar, it is spoken of
> as the Norway rat. It is needless to tell
> our readers that it has long been
> established that the brown rat hails
> from the far East.
>> John S. Roberts, "Genuine
>> Norway Rat" (1873)

ORGANDY

Both "organdy" and "organza"—crisp cotton or silk fabric—come from the town named Urgench (in present-day Uzbekistan in Central Asia). It was on the old Silk Route and was an early market for Chinese silk fabric.

> She wore an organdy dress with lots

of ruffles and flounces in a style that
I later found had been popularized by
an American actress called Deanna
Durbin.
> Ross Thomas, *The Fools in
> Town are on Our Side* (1970)

ORRERY

A mechanical model of the solar system named after the
fourth Earl of Orrery, Charles Boyle (1674-1736), though it
was invented by George Graham in 1731. Orrery is an ancient
territory in Munster, Ireland, represented by the modern
barony of Orrery in the north of the county of Cork.

> After I had made myself master of the use
> of the globes and of the orrery, and
> conceived an idea of the infinity of space,
> and of the eternal divisibility of matter,
> and obtained at least a general knowledge
> of what is called natural philosophy, I
> began to confront, the internal evidence
> those things afford with the Christian
> system of faith.
> > Thomas Paine, *The Age of
> > Reason* (1794)

OXFORD

It can mean a dress shirt woven from Oxford cloth, so named
because its manufacturing process—the "Oxford weave"—
was first developed in Oxford, England. It can also mean a
low-shoe laced over the instep.

> He was wearing what appeared to be his
> overage preppy schoolboy uniform, a navy
> blazer over a light blue oxford shirt, khaki
> slacks, and cordovan tassel loafers.
> > Ellen Byerrum, *Armed and
> > Glamorous* (2008)

P

PAISLEY

The teardrop or tadpole shape pattern, used on a range of goods, is named for a large town in Scotland. It was used on shawls in Kashmir, which were brought back to Britain by the East India Company in the mid-eighteenth century, where they quickly became the vogue. As they were in short supply and expensive, enterprising British textile manufacturers imitated them and sold them for a small fraction of the price. They became so popular that the weaving centers in Edinburgh, Norwich, and Paisley were overcome with orders. For seventy years the patterned shawls remained fashionable, and 'paisley' became globally renowned.

> And here I was, a new face in the snakepit, a pervert yet to be classified, sporting a paisley tie and button-down shirt, no longer young but not quite over the hump—a man on the brink, as it were trotting back to the library to find out what was going on.
> Hunter S Thompson, *The Rum Diary* (1998)

PALACE

A magnificent house in which an emperor, king, or other distinguished person resides. From the Latin *palatium*, so named for the first imperial residence on the Palatium or Palatine Hill, one of the seven hills of Rome, the first that was built upon. The emperor Augustus dwelt there, and many fine palaces were consequently built there.

> A big oil baron of Dallas
> Built a home for his wife, Alice.
> The neighbors complained;
> "Too big," they explained,
> "It's not a house, it's a palace!"

PALM BEACH SUIT

The fabric for the lightweight suit was first produced by the Goodall Mills in Sanford, Maine during the early years of the last century. It was not manufactured in Palm Beach; rather the name suggested that it was the kind of suit one could wear in a climate like the fashionable Florida resort town. Though it was a trademarked name, it soon became used generically for similar summer suits.

> A tall, thin man in what is known
> (excepting at Palm Beach) as a
> "Palm Beach suit," entered the shop.
> Julian Street, *American
> Adventures* (1917)

PANAMA

The hat originated in Ecuador, where the Incas first wove them from palm leaves. During the construction of the Panama Canal, hat sellers started to make what is called *paja toquilla* ("hat made from straw") available to workers, who referred to it as "Panama hast," as that was easier to say than the Spanish name. When Theodore Roosevelt was photographed at the controls of a bulldozer wearing one, the design took off in the

United States and in Britain.

> J.T. was smoking a cigarette, his dark
> panama pulled down to his eyebrows . . .
> Mayra Montera, *Captain of*
> *the Sleepers* (2002)

PARÁ RUBBER

The mother of all rubber trees, the *hevea brasiliensis*, native to tropical America, but now cultivated around the world and the source of commercial rubber. It is named for the northern Brazilian state of Pará.

> It is singular how a name is preserved, for
> Para was the original port of shipment. In
> later years the port became Manaos,
> lthough the name "para" rubber was still
> given to the best grade from Brazil. Not
> only that, but all high-grade rubber is
> colloquially known as "para" rubber.
> The wood from the tree, used in furniture
> manufacturing, is called "parawood."
> William Geer, *The Reign of*
> *Rubber* (1922)

PARCHMENT

The skin of a sheep or goat prepared and rendered fit for writing on. It was invented 198 B.C. by Eumenes II, king of Pergamum, an ancient Greek city in western Asia Minor, as a substitute for papyrus. Over time "Pergamum" became known as "parchment" in English.

> Is not this a lamentable thing, that of the
> skin of an innocent lamb should be
> made parchment? That parchment, being
> scribbled o'er, should undo a man?
> William Shakespeare, *King*
> *Henry VI, Part II* (1592)

PAVANE

A dignified and stately dance that originated in the sixteenth century in Padua, Italy, *Pava* being a dialect name for the city.

> Three years earlier, Lon Nolan had not
> known what a pavane was. Now he was
> dancing one—if not with the grace of a
> sixteenth-century European nobleman,
> at least without tripping over his own
> feet or stepping on anyone else's.
> Rick Shelley, *Captain* (1999)

PEACH

The fruit tree, though native to China, reached Europe by way of Persia (modern-day Iran), where it picked up its name. Originally "Persian apple," from the Greek *Persikon malon.*

> Shall I part my hair behind? Do I
> dare to eat a peach?
> I shall wear white flannel trousers,
> and walk upon the beach.
> I have heard the mermaids singing,
> each to each.
> T. S. Eliot, "The Love Song
> of J. Alfred Prufrock" (1917)

PEKINGESE

There is a Chinese legend from Peking about a lion that fell in love with a marmoset. In order for him to marry her, the lion begged the patron saint of animals to make him the size of a pigmy, but to keep his big lion heart and character. The offspring of this wedding are said to be the dog of Fu Lin, or the Lion Dog of China. This breed is now called Pekingese, "from Peking," the former name of the Chinese capital of Beijing.

A shrill barking precipitated her out of
her high eternity. She opened her eyes
reluctantly and looked around. The
small and silky parody of an extreme-
oriental monster, her little Pekingese
was barking at the kitchen cat.

Aldous Huxley, *Point Counter
Point* (1928)

PERCHERON

This breed of horse derives its name from the place that
spawned it, Le Perche, an old province located some fifty
miles southwest of Paris.

Our host, that Raoul, is roaming
around in a ten-gallon hat, Tom Mix
shirt and a brace of sixguns with a
Percheron horse by the bridle.

Thomas Pynchon,
Gravity's Rainbow (1973)

PERSIAN

"Persian" can refer to a type of domestic cat with long silky
hair, thought to have come from Iran (formerly Persia),
Turkey, and its neighbors. During that 16th century the first
cats of the breed began to arrive in Europe.

Much of Zoe's spare time was spent
indulging her Persian cat, who had a
mahogany-paneled litter box, a selection
of rhinestone collars and a blue velvet
cat bed. Byron was regularly bathed and
groomed, and ate his designer cat food
from china saucers.

Lisa Kleypas, *Rainshadow
Road* (2012)

PHEASANT

From the Greek *phasianos*," literally "Phasian bird," from *Phasis,* a river that flows into the Black Sea in Colchis, in Georgia, where the birds were said to have been plentiful.

> Oh, I've dined off the golden plates and fine
> silver of the crowned heads of Europe, and
> I've et pheasant under glass, but nothing can
> beat a plate full of Texas barbecue down here
> with the people of Pear Orchard.
> Donna Ingham, *1001 Greatest
> Things Ever Said About Texas*
> (2006)

PHILISTINISM

Conventionality devoid of culture; a lowbrow. Apparently, this was how the inhabitants of the ancient Philistine states of Canaan were perceived by their neighbors.

> America has been only too well
> acquainted with the barbarian
> Philistinism of the *nouveau riche.*
> Norman Jacobs, *Mass Media
> in Modern Society* (1959)

PIEDMONT

As an adjective, it means "lying at the foot of a mountain or mountain range." As a noun, it refers to such an area. It literally means "foothill" in French, a translation of *Piemonte,* the region of Italy known in English as the Piedmont.

> In 1713 few Anglo-Americans lived more
> than fifty miles from the Atlantic, but by
> 1750 one-third of the colonists resided in
> the piedmont.
> Paul S. Boyer, *The Enduring
> Vision* (2012)

PIMA

A high-quality cotton developed in Pima County, Arizona, from selected Egyptian cottons.

> "Well, I would like a white shirt . . ." I paused as I pulled out the list of criteria I had written down earlier. "I would like a two-ply pinpoint all-cotton shirt with a thread count of at least 110, made with cotton with a 200-yarn count, and, if possible, made with Egyptian, Sea Island, or pima cotton."
>
> Jay B. Barney, *What I Didn't Learn in Business School* (2010)

PISTOL

A firearm designed for one-hand use. The term is of uncertain origin, but, according to one theory, the pistol owes its name to Pistoia, a town in Tuscany, Italy, where handguns were made as early as the fifteenth century

> Oh, drinkin' beer in a cabaret
> Was I havin' fun!
> Until one night she caught me right
> And now I'm on the run.
> Oh, lay that pistol down, babe.
> Lay that pistol down.,
> Pistol packin' mama
> Lay that pistol down
>
> From "Pistol Packin' Mama" (1943) by Al Dexter

PLASTER OF PARIS

A white gypsum powder that forms a paste when mixed with water, hardening into a solid. It was originally dug at Montmartre, in Paris.

> The Plaster Casters of Chicago, a
> cheerful double act, who immortal-
> ize pop stars' penises in plaster of
> Paris. One of them procures the
> erection, the other prepares the
> alginate. "I appreciate what they
> are doing," says Frank Zappa, "both
> artistically and sociologically.
> Sociologically it's really heavy."
> Cynthia Plaster Caster concurs . . .
> "It's going to be a significant
> element in the revolution."
> > Richard Neville, *Play-*
> > *power* (1971)

POLAND CHINA

This popular breed of pig has nothing to do with Poland or China. It was started in Warren County, Ohio in the mid-nineteenth century when Big China hogs were crossed with other breeds to produce a large pig. "Poland" does not refer to its provenance. It seems that in one area someone used "Poland" to designate the offspring of a particular hog obtained from a Polish-born farmer. Whatever the origin, "Poland China" became the official name in 1872.

> I think the pig is my favorite animal.
> Few things are more satisfactory to me
> than a high-grade Berkshire or Poland
> China pig.
> > Booker T. Washington, *Up*
> > *From Slavery* (1909)

POLKA

From the Czech *polka,* literally, "Polish woman." It may also be an alteration of *pulka,* meaning "half," for the half-steps of Bohemian peasant dances. It was in vogue first in Prague in

1835; it reached London by 1842. **Polka dot**, first recorded in 1884, is named for the dance, for no reason except its popularity.

> I find today that weddings aren't the
> wild fun they used to be because no
> one is racing around the dance floor,
> polka-ing and shouting *shoop-eye,*
> *shoop-eye* at the tops of their lungs.
> Mary-Ann Tirone Smith,
> *Girls of Tender Age: A*
> *Memoir* (2006)

POLONAISE

Polish national dance, from the French for "Polish." It is in moderate 3-4 time and of slow, stately movements. It evolved from peasant and court processions and ceremonies of the late sixteenth century. Chopin, exiled from Poland, expressed his patriotic fervor in the thirteen polonaises he composed.

> The Polonaise is at once the symbol of war
> and love, a vivid pageant of martial splendor,
> a weaving, cadenced, voluptuous dance, the
> pursuit of the shy, coquettish woman by the
> fierce warrior.
> James Huneker, *Chopin* (1900)

POMERANIAN

The breed descended from the Spitz family of dogs, the sled dogs of Iceland and Lapland. It takes its name from the historical region of Pomerania that makes up the southern coast of the Baltic sea (now present-day Germany and Poland), not because it originated there, but because this was most likely where it was bred down to size.

> Fie upon the insipid beauty-dog, this

absurd quadruped, Pomeranian, King
Charles, pug or lap dog, so pleased
with himself that he runs indiscreetly
between the legs or on the knees of a
visitor as if he were sure of pleasing, as
boisterous as a child, as silly as a
beldame, sometimes as snappish and
insolent as a servant.

> Charles Baudelaire, "In Praise
> of Good Dogs" (1869)

PORT

The sweet fortified wine of Portugal is made from the grapes of the Douro Valley in the northern part of the country. It takes its name from the port city of Oporto, where most of the wine was brought to market or export.

> Slothful disorder filled his stable,
> And sluttish plenty decked her table.
> Their beer was strong, the wine was port;
> Their meal was large, their grace was short.
> Matthew Prior, from "An Epitaph"
> (1718)

PORTLAND CEMENT

A form of concrete that resembles Portland stone, a kind of limestone quarried at the Isle of Portland in England.

> Poor Lefty, if he only could have his wishes,
> He'd be at Lindy's eating his favorite dishes.
> But, alas, that is not how it went.
> Fitted in shoes of Portland cement
> He is now swimming with the fishes.

PRUSSIAN BLUE

Deep-blue pigment discovered in 1704 in Berlin, then part of Prussia. **Prussic acid** is obtained from Prussian blue.

In its day, the building must have been marvelous to behold, with its vermilion-lacquered pillars, lintels carved with flower patterns, and beams painted Prussian blue.

Kyoka Izumi, *Japanese Gothic Tales* (1996)

Q/R

QUINCE

The name of the fruit tree (*Cydonia oblonga*) comes from middle-English *qunce*, from the Greek *kudonion*, meaning "from Kudonia," the ancient name for Canea, capital of Crete.

> They dined on mince, and slices of quince
> Which they ate with a runcible spoon;
> And hand in hand, on the edge of the sand,
> They danced by the light of the moon,
> The moon,
> The moon,
> They danced by the light of the moon.
>> Edward Lear, "The Owl and the
>> Pussycat" (1871)

QUONSET HUT

The prefabricated structure used by the Navy during World War II was first manufactured at Quonset Point, Rhode Island.

> The Quonset hut was not made for the
> frozen north. The snow slides off the
> roof, but metal is a lousy insulator. We
> keep the wood stove going day and night.
>> Clive Cussler, *Blue Gold* (2001)

RAGLAN

A "raglan sleeve" has the shoulder seams slanted and extending to the neckline. It was named for FitzRoy Somerset, the First Baron Raglan (1788-1855), most likely because it was designed to fit his coat for the arm he lost at the Battle of Waterloo. Raglan is situated in the county of Monmouthshire in South Wales. The peerage was created in 1852 for Lord Somerset.

> Winter after winter, my sister and I wore
> our mother's hand-knit sweaters—the winter
> white, fisherman-type pullovers with their
> thick cables; the smooth, stocking stitch,
> button-down cardigans with raglan sleeves.
> Colleen Sell, *A Cup of Comfort*
> *for Mothers to Be* (2006)

RHINESTONE

The name of the imitation diamond is a translation of the French *caillou du Rhin*, as it was originally made at Strasbourg, the French city on the Rhine.

> But oh, sometimes I think about you
> And the way you used to ride out
> In your rhinestones and your sequins
> With the sunlight on your hair
> And oh, the crowd will always love you
> But as for me I've come to know
> Everything that glitters is not gold.
> From "Everything That Glitters
> (Is Not Gold) (1985) by Dan Seals

RHUBARB

The plant's name is a descendant of *rha barbaron* ("foreign rhubarb"), from *rha*, "rhubarb" (associated with *Rha*, ancient Scythian name of the River Volga) plus *barbaron*, neuter of *barbaros* "foreign."

> "There's a babe out there somewhere
> who is ready to bake a rhubarb pie for

me, and even wash my dirty laundry
once in a while as part of the deal . . ."
Perri O'Shaughnessy, *Unlucky in Law* (2004)

RITZY

Slang term for fancy or elegant, from the fashionable Ritz hotels—especially New York's Ritz-Carlton—founded by Swiss hotelier César Ritz (1850-1918).

When I take my sugar to tea,
I'm as Ritzy as can be,
'Cause I never take her where
the gang goes,
When I take my sugar to tea.
From "When I Take
My Sugar to Tea"
(1931) by Sammy
Fain *et al.*

ROAM

Scholars disagree about the etymology of this synonym of "wander." Some believe it literally means to "wander to Rome" for the sake of religion. Somehow "Rome" morphed into "roam."

'Mid pleasures and palaces though we
may roam,
Be it ever so humble, there's no place
like home!
John Howard Payne, from
"Home, Sweet Home" (1852)

ROCKAWAY

About 1830 a carriage builder in Jamaica, Long Island, constructed a light four-wheeled horse-drawn wagon with two seats and a standing top. A New York carriage dealer offered the wagons in his showroom. They attracted so much interest that he attempted to keep them as an exclusive item by misleading customers to believe they were built in Rockaway, New Jersey. By the following season the truth about the carriage's builder became known. Though demand was so heavy on the Jamaica carriage builder, the name Rockaway persisted.

> Jean Baptiste Pierre Antoine de Monet,
> Liked to do the Champs in his rockaway.
> He'd stop at a café
> Or at a friend's soiree,
> Then continue to his atelier.

ROMANCE

A term denoting the dialect formerly prevalent in some of the southern districts of France, which springs from Latin—the language of Rome. As songs of chivalry became the most popular compositions in that language, they were called *romans* or *romants*.

> Neither knew nor cared about any
> manifestation of current literature.
> For each there had been no poet later
> than Byron, and neither had read a
> romance since, in childhood, they
> had dipped into the Waverly Novels
> as they appeared in succession.
> Edmund Gosse, *Father*
> *And Son* (1907)

ROTTWEILER

The breed is named after the city of Rottweil, Germany, where they were used to drive cattle to and from the markets and were known as *Rotweiler Metzgerhund* ("butcher dog").

> A well-bred Rotty is good natured and even
> tempered. It is also smart, hardworking
> and sure of itself. Though large, these dog
> are still gentle and playful. They love
> being petted and cuddled by their owner.
> Their owners think Rotties are the best
> dogs. ever!
>> Elaine Landau, *Rottweilers Are*
>> *the Best!* (2003)

RUGBY

A variation of football, named after Rugby School in the town of Rugby in the West Midlands of England, where in 1823 William Webb Ellis—according to the plaque at the school—"with a fine disregard for the rules of football as played in his time, first took the ball in his arms and ran with it, thus originating the distinctive feature of the rugby game."

> Rugby is great. The players don't wear
> helmets or padding; they just beat the
> living daylights out of each other and
> then go for a beer. I love that.
>> Joe Theismann, former NFL
>> Quarterback

S

SAHARA

The world's largest desert is often used as a metaphor for either emptiness or vastness.

> A nation with few serious readers
> is to my mind a Sahara of the spirit.
> Sven Birkerts, *Media Studies*
> *Journal* (1992)

SALUKI

The Saluki, royal dog of Egypt, is perhaps the oldest known domesticated dog. Its image can be found on ancient pottery and crypts throughout the Middle East. Later, the Arabs praised the breed in their poetry, giving it the name *slughi*, "from Saluq," a long-vanished city in South Arabia.

> A tall, grey saluki came out of the house,
> beating his tail against the posts of the
> verandah; "I want one like that," I said,
> "to take up into Persia."
> Vita Sackville-West, *Passenger*
> *to Teheran* (1926)

SAMOYED

The breed was originally developed by the Samoyed people of the tundra lands of the northeastern European Russia and northwestern Siberia. It is derived from the Russian *samoed,* which comes from Lapp *Sāme-Āednama* ("of Lapland").

> Phil arrived in his crew cab pickup
> with the General in the back seat
> smiling at any one who would look
> his way. Actually, the General is a
> Samoyed, and they are also known as
> the "smiling dog" so it wasn't as
> strange as it might seem.
>
> Lawrence Gordon Knudsen,
> *The Clock Struck Intrigue* (2003)

SANDWICH

The modern-day convenience food was created by John Montagu, the fourth Earl of Sandwich (1718-1792). The family of the Earls of Sandwich had no real connection to the town of Sandwich in Kent in southeast England, only the title. The first Earl originally intended to take the title of the Earl of Portsmouth—this may have been changed as a nod to the town of Sandwich, because the fleet he was commanding in 1660 was lying off its shore.

> There was a young man from Ipswich
> Who ate a gigantic sandwich.
> It got stuck in his craw
> And it would not withdraw,
> So they had to do a Heimlich.

SANTANA

Another name for the "Santa Ana," the dry and warm winds in the Southern California area that blow in from the desert. The source for the name is not certain, but it seems likely that it is named for the Santa Ana Canyon in Orange County, California.

There was a desert wind blowing that night.
It was one of those hot dry Santa Anas that
come down through the mountain passes
and curl your hair and make your nerves
jump and your skin itch. On nights like that
every booze party ends in a fight. Meek
little wives feel the edge of the carving
knife and study their husbands' necks.
Anything can happen. You can even get
a full glass of beer at a cocktail lounge.
                    Raymond Chandler, "Red Wind"
                    (1938)

SAPPHIRE

The blue precious gem's name is believed to derive from a

Sanskrit term meaning "precious to the planet Saturn."

Such a play of colors and lights, different
seasons, different hours of the day—the
lines of the far horizon where the faint-
tinged edge of the landscape loses itself
in the sky. As I slowly hobble up the lane
toward day-close, an incomparable sunset
shooting in molten sapphire and gold,
shaft after shaft, through the ranks of the
long-leaved corn, between me and the west.
                    Walt Whitman, *Specimen Days*
                    (1882)

SARDINE

Some believe that the name of the fish is derived from *Sardo*

"Sardinia," the Mediterranean island, near which the fish were

probably caught and from which they were exported.

Oh for the life of a sardine!
That is the life for me!
Cavorting and spawning every morning
Under the deep blue sea.
To have no fear for storm nor gale.
Oh to chase the tail of a whale!

Oh for the life of a sardine!
That is the life for me!
> From "Oh For the Life
> of a Sardine" by Charlie
> Chaplin

SARDONIC

From the Latin *sardonicus,* in *Sardonius risus,* a loan-translation of Greek *sardonios (gelos)* "of bitter or scornful (laughter)," because the Greeks believed that eating a certain plant they called *sardonion* (literally "plant from Sardinia") caused facial convulsions resembling those of sardonic laughter, usually followed by death.

> The forlorn woman had a peculiar face.
> Her smile was no smile. But when in
> repose her features had a shadowy look
> that was like a sardonic grin, as if some
> one had sketched with cruel forefinger
> indelible lines about her mouth
> > Stephen Crane, *Maggie, A
> > Girl of the Streets* (1893)

SATIN

The glossy fabric's name is derived from *Zaytun,* the Arabic form of Chinese *Tseutung,* former name of *Tsinkiang,* the city in southern China, where it was likely first exported.

> Cigarette holder which wigs me
> Over her shoulder, she digs me.
> Out cattin' that satin doll.
> Baby, shall we go out skippin?
> Careful, amigo, you're flippin',
> Speaks Latin that satin doll.
> > From "Satin Doll"
> > Lyrics by Billy Strayhorn

SATURNINE

Glum or taciturn, the temperament of one born under the supposed astrological influence of the planet Saturn.

> With black hair and dark eyes, her looks reflected her saturnine personality growing up. She was a brooder who spent her teenage years locked in her room, listening to gloomy music and writing in her diary.
> Nicholas Sparks, *The Wedding* (2003)

SAUTERNES

The white dessert wine is grown in the Graves district of the Bordeaux region of France. The designated area includes the five communes of Barsac, Bommes, Fargues, Preignac, and Sauternes. "Sauterne" (spelled without the final *s*) is a generic name in the United States for inexpensive white wine, quite different from the famous French sauturnes.

> Mrs. Gerard, who was very proud of her dinners, and never able to resist the temptation of commenting upon them to her guests, leaned across to Presley and Mrs. Cedarquist, murmuring, "Mr. Presley, do you find that Sauterne too cold? I always believe it so *bourgeois* to keep such a delicate wine as Sauterne on the ice, and to ice Bordeaux of Burgundy —oh, it is nothing short of a crime."
> Frank Norris, *The Octopus* (1901)

SCALAWAG

A rascal, a reprobate. There seems to be no agreement among authorities as to the origin of the term, though some claim it originally meant "an undersized, worthless animal," perhaps from "Scalloway," one of the Shetland Islands of Scotland, an allusion to its small ponies.

The Power of the Scalawag

A Forestry commissioner had just felled
a giant tree when, seeing an honest man
approaching, he dropped his axe and fled.
The next day when he cautiously returned
to get his axe, he found the following lines
lines penciled on the stump:

> *What nature reared by centuries*
> *of toil,*
> *A scalawag in half a day*
> *can spoil;*
> *An equal fate for him may*
> *Heaven provide—*
> *Damned in the moment of*
> *his tallest pride.*
> Ambrose Bierce, *Fantastic Fables* (1898)

SCALLION

A young onion before the enlargement of the bulb. Formerly called "Ascalonian onion" because it came from Ascalon, the port in southern Palestine.

> The scallion is not an onion, not a true
> bulb, not a shallot. It is sometimes called
> a green onion or a spring onion. Whatever
> the scallion is, it is a delightful, zesty
> addition to both cooked and raw recipes.
> Barry Ballister, *The Fruit and Vegetable Stand* (2002)

SCHWEINFURT GREEN

The intense, light valued, blue green compound of arsenic and verdigris was discovered in 1814 at Sehweinfurt, Germany, and manufactured under a variety of names—Vienna green, King's green, Paris green, Mitis green, Parrot green, and (in English-speaking countries) emerald green. All these synthetic compounds fell out of use by the mid-twentieth century.

> Imprinted in thick relief on cheap,
> patterned wallpaper, the Schweinfurt
> green, if exposed to damp, decompose
> to release arsine, a deadly gas. . . .
> Legend has it that Napoleon Bonaparte
> died of poisoning from the artificial
> fumes exuded by the emerald green
> paint on the damp walls of his house
> in exile on Saint Helena.
> Philip Ball, *Bright Earth: Art*
> *and the Invention of Color*
> (2003)

SCOTCH

As a noun, "Scotch" is simply short for Scotch whisky, probably Scotland's most famous export. As a verb, it means to hinder or prevent.

> Well, between Scotch and nothin', I
> suppose I'd take Scotch. It's the nearest
> thing to good moonshine I can find.
> William Faulkner

SCOTTIE

The short-legged terrier was developed in the Scottish highlands to hunt vermin that plagued local farmers.

> Twin scotties are quite a sight
> When one's black, the other white.
> —Even better if clad
> In a Scottish plaid—
> A Caledonian delight!

SEALYHAM

The sturdy little terrier derives its name from *Sealy Ham*, Haverfordwest, Wales, the estate of Captain John Edwards, who developed a strain of dog noted for its prowess in quarrying badger, fox, and otter.

> Dogs have never frightened me the
> hundreds of times I have been burgling.
> Those yapping little brutes, Pekingese,
> Sealyhams, and such like, are the worst.
> George Smithson, *Raffles in
> Real Life* (1930)

SEDAN

Originally a portable chair or covered vehicle for carrying one person, and borne on poles by two men. Some claim the word is from the Latin *sedeo*, "to sit," while other hold it comes from the town of Sedan, France, where they were first made. Litters having gone out of style, today the word is used with regard to automobiles.

> Some of the more popular cars on
> Woodward in the early 1960s were the
> 1955 to 1957 Chevy sedans. A used
> sedan was inexpensive to buy and could
> easily be turned into a very fast car with
> the swap of a higher-horsepower small-
> block engine.
> Robert Genat, *Woodward
> Avenue*: (2010)

SELTZER

Seltzer water, or more properly Selter's Water, is named from a spring near the village of Nieder-Selters in Germany.

The seltzer bottle was always near the whiskey.

> Amy was fond of seltzer and whiskey high-balls.
> When she became particularly illuminated, she
> would act quite girlish, and pick up the seltzer
> bottle and squirt some of its contents in my face.
> Jim Tully, *Beggars of Life* (1924)

SEPHARDIM

One of the two principal divisions of Jews (the other is Ashkenazim), usually a Spanish or Portuguese Jew or one of his or her descendants, from *Sepharadh*, Hebrew for "Spain."

> Emma probably identified with Disraeli, whom
> she saw as a Jew in Christian society. More
> significant, however, he was a Sephardic Jew,
> as was she, and he "knew himself to be the
> descendant, not of pariahs and pawnbrokers, but
> of princes, prophets, statesmen, poets, and
> philosophers, and in his veins was kindled that
> enthusiasm of faith in the genius and high
> vocation of his own people, which strikes
> outsiders as an anomaly of a member of an
> habitually despised race."
> Bette Roth Young, *Emma Lazarus
> in Her World* (1997)

SERGE

Twilled cloth of worsted commonly used for suits, from *serikos*, "from Seres," the Greek word for Ch'ins, that is, the Chinese..

> He was dressed for town . . . in a blue
> serge suit, striped cotton shirt, and a pink
> straw with an enameled artificial look.
> Wright Morris, *The Home Place*
> (1984)

SEVRES

A porcelain from Sevres, France, where it is manufactured.

I cannot live with you,
It would be life,
And life is over there
Behind the shelf
The sexton keeps the key to,
Putting up
Our life, his porcelain,
Like a cup
Discarded of the housewife,
Quaint or broken;
A newer Sevres pleases,
Old ones crack.

      From "I Cannot Live With
      You" by Emily Dickinson

SHALLOT

From Latin *escallonia,* meaning "(onion) from Ascalon"
(modern-day Askhelon), an Israeli seaport.

    The French use shallots for seasoning far
    more than onions. In this country, that
    would be prohibitive. Shallots are
    expensive because their growing habit
    makes using machinery impossible—
    people must care for shallots in the field.
        Irma Rombauer, *The Joy of*
        Cooking (rev.1997)

SHANGHAI

"To drug a man unconscious and ship him as a sailor," from
the practice of kidnapping to fill the crews of ships making
extended voyages, such as to the Chinese seaport of Shanghai.

    Those who were shanghaied were not
    usually sailors. One would find tailors,
    sheep-herders, waiters and riff-raff
    of the slums, who had fallen prey to
    the greed of the boarding-house keeper.
        Arthur Mason, *The Flying*
        Bo'sun (1920)

SHANTUNG

A coarse silk from Shantung province, in China, where the
fabric was made.

> He used to fly his Spitfire during the
> Battle of Britain wearing the clothes
> he thought proper for the time of day.
> He once destroyed six German planes
> between ten and eleven in the morning
> dressed in scarlet shantung pajamas,
> sealskin slippers, and a sky blue cashmere
> dressing-gown with silver piping.
>> Harry Matthews, *The*
>> *Conversions* (1997)

SHAWL

A cloth used by women as a loose covering for the neck and
shoulders. Some authorities say the name comes from Shawl,
a town and valley in Baluchistan. now a province of Pakistan.

> Does he live on turnips, tea or tripe,
> Does he like his shawl to be marked
>> with a stripe
>>> or a Dot,
>> The Ahkond of Swat?
>> Edward Lear, from "The
>> Ahkond of Swat" (1851)

SHELTIE

The Sheltie, short for "Shetland Sheepdog," is a herding breed
that originates from the Shetland Islands near Scotland. They
are often called "miniature collies" by the non-initiated, but
they are actually a separate breed.

> I have not seen Jamie for a long time.
> She is a charming dog and brought

back poignant memories of Tamas,
although she is much thinner, thinner boned and smaller, but she has
the wonderful Sheltie face, so loving.
May Sarton, *Encore* (1995)

SHERRY

Along with Cognac and Armagnac in France, Jerez, Spain is
one of only three officially demarcated brandy regions in
Europe. It is in the province of Andalusia, and was originally
named *Caesaris* in honor of Julius Caesar which subsequently
became modified to the more native sounding *Xeres* (now
Jerez), which the English mispronounced *Sherris* and which
they believed to be plural, produced sherry "(wine of) Xeres."

Oh, for a bowl of fat Canary,
Rich Palermo, sparkling Sherry,
Some nectar else, from Juno's dairy;
Oh, these draughts would make us merry!
From "Oh, For a Bowl of Fat
Canary" by John Lyly (1584)

SHETLAND

The pony hails from the Shetland Island in Scotland. Other
"toponymic' ponies include the **Welsh**, the **Connemara** (from
the area of Connaught in Ireland) and the **Chincoteague** (from
the Virginia island of that name).

Maggie was incessantly tossing her
head to keep the dark heavy locks out
of her gleaming black eyes--an action
which gave her very much the air of
a small Shetland pony
George Eliot, *The Mill on
the Floss* (1860)

SIAMESE

The cat is considered by many to be a "natural" breed—one that developed without the intervention of man. Pictures of seal-point Siamese cats appear in the manuscript "Cat-Book Poems," written in Siam (now Thailand) sometime between 1350 and 1700 A.D. **Siamese twins** are conjoined twins, after the Bunker brothers born there in 1811.

> But most to Cats of foreign race his hatred
>   had been vowed;
> To Cats of foreign name and race no quarter
>   was allowed.
> The Persian and the Siamese regarded him
>   with fear—
> Because it was a Siamese had mauled his
>   missing ear.
>   From "Growltiger's Last Stand"
>   (1939) by T.S. Eliot

SIENNA

A clay used as a pigment for painting, such as raw sienna or burnt sienna, from Italian *terra di Sienna,* "earth of Siena," a city in Tuscany in central Italy.

> I had long been familiar with a paint in
> my color-box called Burnt Sienna, and
> was now much interested to learn that
> it was made in the yellow clay on
> which the city of Siena stands.
>   Julian Hawthorne, *Hawthorne*
>   *and His Circle* (1903)

SILK

A lustrous fabric produced by silkworms. The word can be traced back to the Greek-Latin word *Seres*, for the Ch'ins, that is, the Chinese. from whom silk was first obtained.

I have wrapped my dreams in a silken cloth,
And laid them away in a box of gold;
Where long will cling the lips of the moth;
I have wrapped my dreams in a silken
        cloth;
I hide no hate, I am not even wroth
Who found earth's breath so keen and cold;
I have wrapped my dreams in a silken
        cloth,
And laid them away in a box of gold.
        Countee Cullen, "For a Poet" (1929)

SINOLOGY

The study of Chinese language or culture. "Sino" is from the Greek *Sinai*, "Chinese," which is derived from the Mandarin *Ch'in*, the dynastic name of the country.

        "A Sinologist is someone who
studies China."
        I detected a lot of wariness.
Dylan's crowd all waited too long a time
to respond, and when they did they did
it all at once.
        "What, like pottery and plates
you mean?"
        "That's a very fancy word."
        "Dinner services?"
        I couldn't tell whether they were
laughing at me or not. I had to assume they
were not.
        "China. Its history and culture.
Chinese civilization is what a Sinologist
studies. Not dinner services."
        David Flusfeder, *The Gift*
        (2003)

SISAL

A fiber used for rope, from the sisal plant, after Sisal, a town in Mexico's Yucatan peninsula.

> We walked to a whitewashed shack where
> a young woman sold rice and black beans
> from the same sisal mat where she slept
> with her husband.
>> Edwige Danticat, *Breath, Eyes,*
>> *Memory* (1998)

SKID ROW

The source of the term is thought to have originated in either Vancouver or Seattle, where it was adapted from the term "skid road," used to skid logs through woods. Loggers spent the summers in the mountains; in the winter when out-of-work, they would gather on Skid Road looking for work and would often run out of money, sleep on the streets, and find themselves reduced to begging. Thus the connection between skidding logs and being poor and unemployed.

> Here's a story about a sinner,
> He used to be a winner who enjoyed a life of
>> prominence and position,
> But the pressures at the office and his socialite
>> engagements,
> And his selfish wife's fanatical ambition,
> It turned him to the booze,
> And he got mixed up with a floosie
> And she led him to a life of indecision.
> The floosie made him spend his dole
> She left him lying on Skid Row
> A drunken lag in some Salvation Army Mission.
> It's such a shame.
>> From "Alcohol" (1971), lyrics
>> by Ray Davies of The Kinks

SLEAZY

Since the 17th century, it has meant "flimsy" or "insubstantial." Though its origin is not certain, it may come from *Silesian,* "of Silesia," once an eastern province of Germany that manufactured inexpensive fabrics. The sense of "squalid" did not appear until 1941 and its back-formation into the noun "sleaze" started showing up in the late 1960s.

> Adjectives are a dime a dozen,
> modifying and qualifying stronger
> terms, but nouns--especially the
> short, punchy affixing a –ness can
> define an era. Take sleazy, an adjective
> that was just poking along (originally
> a slur on cheap products from Silesia)
> until it was given a quick haircut to
> become the noun sleaze. Its usage
> exploded in 1980 into the political
> "age of sleaze," a phrase for petty
> corruption that replaced a previous
> generation's "mess in Washington."
> William Safire, *New York Times* (2005)

SODOMY

"Unnatural acts" such as were presumed prevalent in the ancient Canaanite city of Sodom and its sister city, Gomorrah, that led to their destruction by fire, according to *Genesis.*

> The world is full of double beds
> And most delightful maidenheads,
> Which being so, there's no excuse
> For sodomy or self-abuse.
> Hilaire Belloc, (1870-1953)

SOLECISM

The meaning of a nonstandard usage or grammatical construction has been widened to mean any impropriety or mistake. It refers to the corrupt Attic dialect spoken by Athenian colonists at Soloi, in Cilicia.

> Her English is good, apart from a few
> stubborn idiosyncrasies of preposition
> and tense, but these are music to me,
> sung solecisms—how else to describe
> "I am already loving you," her first
> declaration of feeling for me? . . .
>> Ronan Bennett, *The*
>> *Catastrophist* (1997)

SOLFERINO

A shade of purple, it was with named after a famous battle.

The dye was developed in the year of the Battle of Solferino in

1859. Solferino is a village in the Lombardy region of Italy.

> Both of these girls were in gay apparel; one
> was clad in a skirt of brilliant solferino purple
> hue with a black silk waist lavishly trimmed
> with large jet beads.
>> George Wharton Edwards, *London* (1922)

SORGHUM

A kind of grass cultivated as grain and as a syrup source, from

the Latin *syricum (granum),* "Syrian (grass)." Most likely

Syria was the ancient source of the plant.

> "We'll have enough cane left fer to run off
> the last batch of sorghum before the dance,"
> says Fronnie. "The young and the old can
> git around the sorghum pan with their sticks
> and lick the foam from the pan. We ust to
> do that when we's girls. Lord, I can re-
> member the good times we had! We didn't
> mind the work when we made sorghum
> molasses. We thought about the good time
> we's goin to have when we finished makin,
> the molasses."
>> Jesse Stuart, *Trees of Heaven*
>> (1980)

SPA

Either a mineral spring or resort area where such springs exist. It is named for the resort town of that name in eastern Belgium where the wealthy went to "take the waters."

> She looked good, relaxed, like after a
> day at the spa.
> > Marcus Sakey *At the City's
> > Edge* (2009)

SPANIEL

Some credit Spain as the origin of these hunting dogs, with the name being derived from the French word for "Spaniard," itself with roots in "Hispania," the Roman name for the Iberian peninsula.

> He was medium height and stocky with
> bushy eyebrows mounted over brown
> cocker spaniel eyes.
> > Lawrence Block, *A Ticket to
> > the Boneyard* (1991)

SPARTAN

From *Sparta,* capital of Laconia, famed for the severity of its social order, the frugality of its people, the valor of its army, and the brevity of its speech.

> He was a man of Spartan habits, and at
> sixty was scrupulous about his diet at
> your table, excusing himself by saying
> the he must eat sparingly and fare hard,
> as became a soldier, or one who was
> fitting himself for difficult enterprises.
> > Henry David Thoreau, "A Plea
> > for Captain Brown" (1859)

SPRUCE

The evergreen tree's formal name is "Spruce fir," meaning "Prussian fir," spruce being an alteration of "of Pruce" from Old French for "Prussia."

> What this man brought in a cotton sack
> Was gum, the gum of the mountain spruce.
> He showed me lumps of the scented stuff
> Like uncut jewels, dull and rough.
> It comes to market golden brown;
> But turns to pink between the teeth.
> Robert Frost, The Gum-gatherer"
> (1916)

STOCKHOLMING

Also called "Stockholm Syndrome," it is a phenomenon in which a hostage begins to identify with to his or her captor, from an incident in the Swedish capital in 1973 where four people were held by bank robbers and came to believe that the latter were protecting them from the police. After their release one hostage became engaged to one of the captors, another started a defense fund.

> I questioned why we had chosen to marry
> each other. Was it because of our strong
> trauma bond from past ops? Was I Stock-
> holming with Bill, marrying him an draw-
> ing close to him so that his CIA-loyal parts
> wouldn't hurt me?
> Kathleen Sullivan, *Unshackled*
> (2003)

STOGIE

The six-horse Conestoga wagons that hauled freight during the late eighteenth/early nineteenth centuries, were named for the Conestoga River Valley, Lancaster County, Pennsylvania, where they originated. As the teamsters liked to smoke cigars during the haul, a cigar maker in Washington, Pennsylvania. manufactured a cheap cheroot, the "Conestoga Cigar." The drivers snatched them up at four for a penny. The brand name was soon lost and the teamsters started to refer to the as "stogies."

> O, yes, I'll agree that a good cigar
> Just after a meal is great;
> Or even a pipe would do me at times,
> And I wouldn't hesitate
> To light up a stogie when pipes are shy;
> Or, if stogies are hard to get,
> Perhaps, for the sake of a smoke, I'd up
> And tackle a cigarette.
> From "On Smoking," by
> Rowland C. Bowman (1904)

STOICAL

Seemingly indifferent to pleasure or pain, imperturbable, from the Greek school of philosophy founded by Zeno in the fourth century B.C. It took its name from *Stoa Poikile* ("painted porch" in Greek) at Athens, a hall near the Agora, where his followers came to hear him lecture.

> He was stoical, serious, austere;
> a dreamer of stern dreams; humble
> and haughty, like all fanatics.
> Victor Hugo, *Les Miserables*
> (1862)

SUEDE

A soft-surfaced leather. It is the French name for "Sweden" and originated in *gants de suede* "(gloves of) Sweden," When the English imported them, it got shortened to just "suede."

It's peculiar. Very peculiar. She says to
me at seven minutes to nine this morning,
"Beauperhuis, "I'm going to buy a pair
of suede gloves." Now it's quarter to ten at
night, and she still isn't back. How can it
take twelve hours fifty-two minutes to buy
a pair of suede gloves? Unless you go to
Sweden.

> Eugène Labiche & March-Michel,
> *An Italian Straw Hat* (1851)

SUNNY

Genial or cheerful, such as a sunny disposition or smile. The

Latin word for sun, "Sol," is the basis for **solar**.

> O soul-enchanting poesy,
> Thou'st long been all the world with me;
> When poor, they presence grows my wealth,
> When sick, thy visions give me health,
> When sad, thy sunny smile is joy
> And was from e'en a tiny boy
>> *From The Progress of Rhyme*
>> (1830) by John Clare

SURREY

The two-seater carriage was first built in Surrey, a county in

the southeast of England. It was introduced to the United

States in the 1870s.

> He'd reserved a surrey with leather
> curtains to be rolled down later, as
> circumstances warranted. Some
> women tended to doubt a gent's
> motives when he trimmed lamps or
> rolled down curtains too early in
> the game, bless their shy little natures.
>> Tabor Evans, *Longarm and
>> the Haunted Whorehouse*
>> (2002)

SWISS

A sheer fabric used for light clothing and curtains, first made on hand looms in Switzerland. "Dotted swiss" is embellished with embroidered or woven dots.

> Catherine Goodhouse was one of those petite doll-like women given to lavender sachets and dresses made from organdy or dotted swiss. Every time she came to Golden Gardens she looked and smelled like spring itself.
> Richard Selzer, *The Doctor Stories* (1996)

SYBARITE

A person devoted to pleasure," literally an "inhabitant of *Sybaris,*" the ancient Greek town in southern Italy whose inhabitants were noted for their love of luxury.

> The citizens of ancient Sybarus
> Were known to be libidinous.
> They took leisure and pleasure
> In equal good measure
> And left the labor to the rest of us.

T

TABBY

A rich water silk, it is often used for a type of cat with like markings. The silk originated in Attabe, near Baghdad.

> 'Twas on a lofty vase's side,
> Where China's gayest art had dyed
>> The azure flower that blow,
> Demurest of the tabby kind,
> The pensive Selima, reclined,
>> Gazed on the lake below.
>> Thomas Grey, from "On the
>> Death of a Favorite Cat" (1746)

TAMARIND

A tropical tree and its edible fruit, from the Arabic *tamra'l hind*, "the date of Hind" or India.

> Has thou not dragged Diana from her car?
>> And driven the hamadryad from the wood
> To seek a shelter in some happier star?
>> Hast thou not torn the Naiad from her flood,
> The Elfin from the green grass, and from me
> The summer dream beneath the tamarind tree?
>> Edgar Allan Poe, from "Sonnet—
>> To Science" (1829)

TANGERINE

The name of the little citrus stems from *tangerine orange,* "an orange from *Tangier,"* the seaport in northern Morocco, from which it was originally exported to Britain.

Picture yourself on a boat in a river
With tangerine trees and marmalade
      skies.
Somebody calls you, you answer
      quite slowly.
A girl with kaleidoscope eyes.
      From "Lucy in the Sky
      with Diamonds" by
      Lennon & McCartney

TANZANITE

The blue gem was discovered in Tanzania in 1967 and given its name by an executive of Tiffany & Co.

      "What is that jewelry you
are wearing?"
      "Tanzanite."
      "Give me diamonds, rubies,
and emeralds."
      Julie was irritated but spoke
sweetly.
      "Tanzanite is mined only in
Tanzania. There is a very limited
amount, which makes it one of the
rarest stones on earth."
      Hilary opened her mouth,
and then closed it.
      Christy Carroll, *Amboseli
Wimbo* (2006)

TARANTULA

The large hairy spider gets its name from a similar creature, *Lycosa tarentula*, of southern Europe, once common in Taranto, in southern Italy. Its bite was once thought to cause **tarantism**, a malady characterized by an uncontrollable urge to dance. The lively dance, the **tarantella**, was once thought to be a remedy for tarantism.

> He looked about as inconspicuous
> as a tarantula on a slice of angel
> food cake.
>> Raymond Chandler

TASMANIAN DEVIL

The world's largest surviving carnivorous marsupial is native to Tasmania. Its spine-chilling screeches, reputed bad temper, and black color led the early European settlers to call it "the Devil."

> He attacked Taylor liker a Tasmanian
> devil, swinging left-handed and right-
> handed haymakers, many of them
> missing, but many landing on
> Tayor's face and body.
>> Nolan Dalla, *One of a
>> Kind* (2005)

TELEMARK

A type of downhill turn performed on cross-country skis in which the knees are bent, the inside heel is lifted, and the weight is on the outside ski. It is named after the county of Telemark in southeastern Norway.

> Clark was fond of competing
> In cross-country skiing.
> "Very nice telemark,"
> The crowd would remark,
> As downhill he was speeding.

TENDERLOIN

An area of a city notorious for its vice. The original Tenderloin was a district south of 42nd Street on Manhattan's west side, full of bordellos and theaters. Because of the reputation of the tenderloin as the choicest cut of beef, it became a metaphor for the best assignment for a crooked cop during the latter part of the nineteenth century.

> He glides easily into a dissipated existence
> in the city's tenderloin district, distinguish-
> ing himself from the hordes of gambling
> fanatics among whom he lives by his talent
> for playing ragtime
> > Lawrence R. Rogers, *Canaan*
> > *Bound* (2005)

TEQUILA

The Mexican liquor, distilled from the fermented juices obtained from the hearts of blue agave plants, gets its name from the town of Tequila located in the state of Jalisco where production started more than 200 years ago.

> Tequila. This spirit made from cactus
> has been used for centuries to promote
> sexual desire. Or at least break down
> inhibitions. Remember that party
> in your sophomore year? No? That's
> Tequila at work.
> > Tilly Rivers, *Erotica*
> > *Café* (2005)

TEXAS HOLD 'EM

There is no definitive trail back to when this popular form of poker was first played, but it did occur, it would seem, in Texas, in the early 1900s. A group of professional card players from the Lone Star state introduced it to Las Vegas at the time it became a popular gambling center.

> One of the many reasons I love no-limit-
> Texas Hold 'Em is I find the balance
> between luck, skill, and bluffing a useful

metaphor for life.

Norman Mailer & John Buffalo
Mailer, *The Big Empty* (2006)

TIGER

Some believe that the fierce cat was named from its frequenting the banks of the Tigris River in modern-day Iraq. The six subspecies are definitely toponyms: The **Royal Bengal**; the **Indochinese** (aka "Corbett's Tiger" after British hunter Jim Corbett [1875-1955]); the **Malayan**; the **Sumatran**; the **Siberian** (aka "the **Amur**" after the river of that name on the Russian/Chinese border); and the **South China** (aka "the **Xiamen**," after the city in Fujian province.)

There was a young lady of Niger,
Who smiled as she rode on a tiger.
They returned from the ride
With the lady inside
And a smile on the face of the tiger.
Anonymous

TOILE DE JOUY

It literally means "cloth from Jouy-en-Josas," in north-central France, where in 1760 one of the first factories to make colorful prints in France was built. They came to be known as "toile de Jouy," or Jouy linen. They became so popular that the French queen Marie Antoinette decorated Versailles with them.

I had no idea what toile de Jouy looked
like, but the name alone alarmed me. . . .
Toile de Jouy did not sound like the
sort of fabric on which one could safely
eat pizza, drink champagne, or do any
of the other fascinating but untidy

things one can do on a sofa.

> Donna Andrews, *Crouching
> Buzzard, Leaping Loon*
> (2004)

TOLUENE

One of the chemicals constituting the explosive TNT—
TriNitroToluene. It refers to the tolu balsam (from which it
was first obtained in 1841) from Santiago de Tolú, Colombia.

> Explosives can be generally classed
> into two types—"slow" (or "push")
> and "fast" (or "burning"). TNT is a
> a "slow" explosive. That is, its primary
> destruction mechanism is the shock
> wave or "front" of explosive gases
> created during detonation.
>
> Tom Clancy, *Special Forces*
> (2001)

TRAVERTINE

A variety of limestone that has a light color and takes a good
polish; it is often used for walls and interior decorations in
public buildings. The word is the French form of the Italian
travertine, an alteration of the Latin (*lapis*) *tiburinus*, (stone)
of Tibur, the ancient name for the town of Tivoli, near Rome,
Italy.

> Travertine was extensively employed
> by the Romans, especially before the
> introduction of marble, for all building
> purposes as also for sarcophagi. . . . It
> s sufficient to mention the Coliseum
> as a proof of its durability.
>
> Mary W. Porter, *What Rome
> was Built with* (1907)

TROY

A traditional system of weight in the British Isles based on the grain, pennyweight (24 grains), ounce (20 pennyweights), and pound (12 ounces). The troy grain, pennyweight, and ounce have been used since the Middle Ages to weigh gold, silver, and other precious metals and stones. The name supposedly derives from the city of Troyes in France, site of one of the major medieval trade fairs.

> Whomever you deal with, use the following standards of measurement to be certain that you're getting what you bargained for. Gold and silver are weighted in troy ounces. There are 31 grams to a troy ounce, and there are 480 grains to a troy ounce. It can be dangerous to confuse grains and grams and ounces.
> Robert S. Rosefsky,
> *Personal Finance* (2002)

TURKEY

The bird with the red wattle was at one time supposed to have come from Turkey. It is, however, a native of America.

> For dinner we had turkey and blazing pudding, and after dinner the Uncles sat in front of the fire, loosened all buttons, put their large most hands over their watch chains, groaned a little and slept.
> Dylan Thomas, *A Child's Christmas in Wales* (1955)

TURQUOISE

The blue/green gemstone was first found in Turkestan and was called "Turkish stone" or *turquois* in French.

Here's a turquoise chain
Of sun-shower rain
To wear if you wish;
And glittering green
With aquamarine,
A silvery fish.

> Elinor Wylie, from "The
> Fairy Goldsmith" (1921)

TUXEDO

The dinner jacket first became popular at a country club in

Tuxedo Park, New York.

> After six o'clock a gentleman is
> expected to appear in full evening
> dress suit, except on occasions when
> the Tuxedo coat is permissible. It
> can be worn at a stag theatre party, a
> club or stag dinner, at summer dinners
> even when women are present, at
> seashore hotels, etc.
>
> *Correct Social Usage* (1906)

TWEED

A soft thick fabric, woven from contrasting woolen yarns, for

coats and suits for both men and women, owes it's name to the

traditional woolen mills alongside the river Tweed in

Scotland.

> Got my tweed pressed, got my best
> vest, all I need now is the girl;
> Got my striped tie, got my hopes high—
> Got the time and the place and I've got
> the rhythm,
> Now all I need's the girl to go with 'em.
>
> From "All I Need is the Girl"
> (1969) lyrics by Stephen
> Sondheim

TYRIAN PURPLE

Also known as royal purple, it is mentioned in texts dating about 1600 BC. It was produced from the mucus of the hypobranchial gland of various species of marine molluscs, notably murex. It originated in the Phoenician city of Tyre, now in Lebanon.

> The ink with which I seek to tell this tale is not, it is true, the majestick tyrian purple
> ... that dye the ancients obtained from shellfish, squeezing the pus that purpled in sunlight from a small cyst behind the whelk's head, a dye so precious that only the richest & most powerful could afford robes of this colour.
>
> Richard Flanagan, *Gould's Book of Fish* (2002)

U/V

ULSTER

The men's overcoat—loose, long, and heavy—is named after Ireland's northernmost province, where they were first made.

> He thought what a trio they must make,
> the two hunched in their smoke-
> colored plastic coats and him huge in
> his old-fashioned ulster and black hat.
> Benjamin Black,
> *Christine Falls* (2006)

ULTIMA THULE

Literally "the most remote Thule," it was used by Latin poets on account of its distance from Rome, to the island of Thule, the existence of which is obscure. The phrase is now poetically applied to the extreme limit of any pursuit.

> Here in the ultima Thule of my mind,
> I no longer think of you. I left you in
> my sleep,
> in the throne I established for you there.
> Julianne Buchsbaum, from
> "Queen of Ultima Thule" (1999)

UMBER

A natural brown earth used as a pigment. It is short for *terre d'Umbre*, "earth of Umbria," a region of central Italy. Or is it?

Some believe that it is not derived from geography, but from the Latin *ombra*, shadow.

> For the somber palette there is nothing
> to match the profundity of umber. Darker
> than sienna pigments owing to a liberal
> proportion of manganese among the
> iron oxide, umber found its way into
> European painting around the end of
> the fifteenth century.
> > Philip Ball, *Bright Earth:*
> > *Art and the Invention of*
> > *Color* (2003)

VALANCE

An ornamental drapery hung across the top of a window or along a shelf, canopy, or bed. It is probably named after Valence, a textile town in southeastern France where the material for such drapery was first manufactured.

> A valance went 'round the bed.
> A deep red with golden thread.
> She slept soundly
> And profoundly
> Beneath the warming bedspread.

VALENCIENNES

A fine type of lace originally manufactured at Valenciennes in north-central France, near the border with Belgium.

> She had sat brushing her hair that
> hung a curtain of black against the
> sheer white dotted swiss of her
> *Gabrielle* with its ruffled lace edging
> of Valenciennes. She wielded the
> silver-backed brush and sniffed the
> air delicately and half closed her eyes.
> "A house isn't really a house," she
> murmured, "unless it has about it the

scent of a good cigar after breakfast."
Edna Ferber, *Saratoga
Trunk* (1941)

VALERIAN

Any of the various plants of the genus *Valeriana*, the roots of one of which is used medicinally as a sedative. The name comes from the Latin *Valerianus*, "of Valeria," a Roman province (included parts of present-day Croatia and Hungary) where the plant supposedly originated.

> I had started drinking valerian tea
> because it helped put me to sleep. Every
> time I woke up, I would drink a cup of
> hot valerian tea and take a few pills that
> would make me feel better, or at least
> put me to sleep for a few more hours.
> Evon Davis, *Pandora's Box*
> (2002)

VARNISH

The paint used to coat a surface with a glossy film takes its name from the Latin *vernix*,"odorous resin," which, in turn, is probably derived from the Greek *Berenike*, the name of an ancient city in Libya (modern Bengasi) credited with the first use of varnishes. The town is named for Berenike II, queen of Egypt, called "Berenice" in English. As a verb it has also come to mean "to gloss over" the truth.

> A recent survey estimated that one in three
> people "varnish the truth" or engage in out-
> and-out lying when seeking employment.
> Charles V. Ford, *Lies, Lies, Lies:
> The Psychology of Deceit* (1996)

VATICAN

The residence of the Roman Catholic pope in Vatican City is a metonymy for the papacy in general. The city is named for Vatican Hill on which it stands, a name which predates Christianity.

> The Vatican was financially rich and innovative in the 1960s—it controlled Immobiliare Roma, which built the Watergate Hotel in Washington-- and Euromerica [which it partnered with Morgan Stanley] the first American-style investment bank it Italy.
>
> Ron Chernow, *The House of Morgan* (2001)

VAUDEVILLE

The name for the once popular stage variety entertainment comes from the French *chanson du Vau de Vire*, a type of satirical song popular in the Valley of Vire, a region of Normandy. "Vau de Vire" became, by corruption, "vaudeville."

> The elements that went into vaudeville were combed from the four corners of the world., There wee hypnotists, iron-jawed ladies, one-legged dancers, one-armed cornetists, mind readers, female impersonators, male impersonators, Irish comedians, Jewish comedians, blackface, German, Swedish, Italian and rube comedians. Vaudeville asked only that you own an animal or an instrument, or have a minimum of talent or a maximum of nerve. With these dubious assets, vaudeville offered fame and riches. It was up to you.

Fred Allen, *Much Ado About
Me* (1956)

VERDIGRIS

There are two forms. The familiar one—the copper carbonate
that discolors copper cookware and gives bronze statuary its
green patina—and the less familiar one—the cultivated copper
acetate caused by the action of acetic acid on copper that was
used in dyes, paints, and medicines. The word literally means
"green of Greece" from the old French *vert-de-Grice*. The
connection with Greece is not known.

> All the time in the bar, and now on
> the steps, he remained astonished by
> her, enthralled by her verdigris eyes . . .
> Michael B. Oren, *Reunion*
> (2003)

W/X/Y/Z

WALL STREET

Manhattan street that is home to the N. Y. Stock Exchange. In the general sense, it means American financial interests.

> He was a familiar Wall Street type, brilliant
> in his grasp of the latest financial exotica yet
> so smitten that he promoted it without regard
> to the underlying economics.
> Roger Lowenstein, *The End of Wall Street* (2010)

WARDOUR STREET ENGLISH

In the 19th century Wardour Street in London's west end was used by dealers in antiques, and "Wardour Street English" was a sort of pseudo-archaic English used by historical novelists, later known as `Tushery' (from "Tush!" as an exclamation).

> He loves to thrust a slang phrase or a crude
> fact in among Wardour Street English ("With
> a hollow groan Ukridge borrowed five
> shillings from me and went out into the night") . . .
> George Orwell, "In Defence of P. G.
> Wodehouse," *Collected Essays* (1968)

WATERLOO

A crushing defeat, as in "meeting one's Waterloo." It is named for Napoleon's disastrous defeat at Waterloo in Belgium in 1815.

> Though Lloyd Webber eventually met
> his Waterloo with *Whistle Down the*
> *Wind,* which closed before ever
> reaching Broadway, the carnage he
> left in his wake could not be undone,
>> Joe Queenan, *Queenan*
>> *Country* (2005

WEIMARANER

The product of selective German breeding, it came from the same general stock which has produced a number of Germany's hunting breeds. In its early days it was known simply as the Weimar Pointer, its name deriving from the noblemen of the Court of Weimar who developed the breed to hunt large game.

> Any person smart enough and strong
> willed enough to properly select, train
> and manage a Weimaraner is in for an
> unparalleled dog-owning experience.
> The owner who overrates himself or
> underrates his Weimaraner is in for
> an ordeal,
>> Roger A Caras, *The Roger*
>> *Caras Dog Book* (1996)

WELLINGTONS

The Wellington boot, also known as a welly, a wellie, a topboot, a gumboot. or a rubber boot, is a type of boot based upon Hessian boots. Wellington is a small industrial town in rural Somerset, England, near the border with Devon. It gave its name to the first Duke of Wellington, Arthur Wellesley, who in turn gave the boot its name as it was a signature part of his uniform. Another English boot is the ankle-high **Chelsea boot**, which had previously been known as jodhpur or paddock boot, likely became known as the Chelsea after the fashionable area of London frequented by mods in the 1960s who adopted as an essential part of their gear. .

> Over the walls and spiked fences giant
> flowering shrubs lie in brilliant mantles.
> Gardeners in blue boiler suits and
> Wellington boots are already at work.
> The air smells summery, of cut grass
> and the diesel of lawnmowers.
> Ronan Bennett, *The
> Catastrophist* (1997)

WELSH

As a verb it means to swindle out of money, especially on a bet; he who welshes is a "welsher." It is not absolutely certain that the words are connected to Wales, but the probability seems to support the connection. So take care when in Wales or with Cambrian-Americans, and consider expunging the words from your vocabulary.

> His money had a habit of putting the
> other fellow in the wrong either way;
> making a liar out of him or showing
> him up for a welsher.
> Cornell Woolrich, "You Bet
> Your Life" (1937)

WHITE HOUSE

The residence and office of the President of the United States is a metonymy for the President and his staff. Other Washington toponyms include "**the Beltway**" (the road that rings the city and stands for the federal government), "**K Street**" (refers to lobbyists and political consultants many of whom have their offices there), and **"the Pentagon"** (meaning the Department of Defense).

> **White House** Do not personify it with phrases such as *the White House said.* Instead, use a phrase such as *a White House official said.*
> *The Associated Press Style-Book* (2004)

WIENER

A shortening of *wienerwurst* (1889), from the German *Wiener* "of Vienna" + *Wurst* "sausage").

> There was a woman, tiny as an elf,
> Who ate a foot-long frank all by herself.
> If I hadn't seen her
> Scarf all of that wiener
> I wouldn't believe it myself.

WORSTED

Woolen yarn made from large-staple yarn, first made in Worthstede (now Worsted), a village in Norfolk, England.

> When I was a small boy at the beginning
> of the century I remember an old man who
> wore knee-breeches and worsted stockings,
> and who used to hobble about the street of
> our village with the help of a stick.
> Samuel Butler, *The Way of All Flesh* (1903)

YAPOK

Also known as a "water opossum," it is the only true aquatic marsupial. Native to Central and South America, it is named after the Oyapock River, the border between French Guiana and Brazil.

Pick any Seussian invention and nature will
equal it. In Dr. Seuss's *McElligot's Pool*
there's a fish with a kangaroo pouch. Could
there be such a fish in the real world? Not a
fish, maybe, but in South America there is
an animal called the yapok—a wonderfully
Seussian name—that takes its young for a
swim in a waterproof pouch.

> Chet Raymo, "Dr. Seuss and Dr.
> Einstein: Children's Books and
> Scientific Investigation" (1992)

YTTRIUM

The little Swedish village of Ytterby has distinguished itself as
the place where four elements—yttrium, **ytterbium**, **erbium**,
and **terbium**—were discovered and after which they were
named.

Yttrium is often classified as one of the
rare earth elements because it is found in
all rare earth minerals and it is very like
them chemically. Even so, it is not one
of this group, and it is certainly not rare,
being twice as abundant as lead.

> John Emsley, *Nature's Building
> Blocks* (2011)

INDEX

Cairngorm	42
Calico	43
California roll	43
Californium	84
Calvados	44
Cambric	44
Campanile	44
Canada goose	44
Canary	45
Canopy	46
Cantaloupe	46
Canter	46
Cape Cod	47
Capeskin	47
Capitol	48
Capris	48
Cardigan	48
Casaba	49
Cashmere	49
Catacombs	49
Caucasian	50
Cedar of Lebanon	50
Chambray	51
Champagne	51
Chantilly lace	51
Charlatan	52
Charleston	52
Charolais	82
Chartreuse	53
Chelsea boot	181
Cherry	53
Chesterfield	54
Chestnut	54
Cheviot	55
China	55
Chinoiserie	55
Chihuahua	55
Chincoteague	155
Christiana	56
Cilice	56
Clydesdale	56
Coach	57
Coffee	57
Cognac	58
Cologne	58
Conga	58
Conga drum	58
Connemara	155
Copper	59
Cordovan	59
Corinthian	60
Corinthian order	60
Coton de Tulear	60
Cravat	61

Kersey	96
Kremlin	96
Krimmer	97
Labrador retriever	97
Laconic	98
Landau	98
Langley	99
Lateen	99
Latin	99
Lavaliere	100
Leghorn	101
Lesbian	101
Lhasa apso	102
Limerick	102
Limoges	107
Limousin	82
Limousine	103
Linsey-Woolsey	103
Lisle	104
Lovage	104
Lumber	104
Lunatic	105
Lyme disease	105
Lyonnaise	106
Mackinaw	107
Maine-Anjou	82
Madeira	107
Madison Avenue	108
Madras	108
Madrilene	108
Maffick	109
Magenta	109
Magnesium	110
Magnet	109
Majolica	110
Malayan tiger	170
Malines	110
Mall	111
Malmsey	111
Maltese	112
Manhattan	112
Manganese	110
Manila	113
Manx	113
Marathon	113
Marburg virus	71
Marsala	114
Martingale	114
Maudlin	115
Mazurka	115
Meander	116
Mecca	116
Mechlin	110
Meissen ware	111